CATS
V.
CONNIFF

**A chronicle of the historic lawsuit brought against
Frank Conniff by his cats, Millie & Barney**

Published By
Podhouse 90 Press
ISBN: 978-0-692-84587-5

Design, Typesetting, Illustrations and Cover Design by Len Peralta

Dedicated to Teresa Strasser,
who brought both Millie and Barney into my life
(much to Millie and Barney's chagrin, no doubt),
and to John Fugelsang, who helped me transport the cats
from Los Angeles to New York City,
giving them the opportunity to be pissed-off
in an entirely different part of the country.

CHAPTER ONE

Some already knew about Frank Conniff from his work as a writer and performer on TV shows like *Mystery Science Theater 3000*. Others knew him as a stand-up comedian. Most people never heard of him and were happy to keep it that way. But now, if he has any fame at all, it is from his involvement in a notorious, precedent-setting legal case that caught the attention of animal lovers the world over. When people used to recognize Mr. Conniff, they'd say things like, *"Hey, aren't you the guy that was in that thing?"* or, *"Hi, I'm a big fan of people you've worked with!"* or, *"Stop bothering me, I have no idea who you are and I don't want your autograph!"* But now he is genuinely famous and most people who accost him on the street almost always say the same thing, *"Hey, aren't you the douchebag who was sued by his cats?"*

It was a case he lost in the court of public opinion right from the start. Defamation of Character is a serious charge, and when it's leveled by two tiny, fluffy creatures, many couldn't help but feel that Conniff must have done something wrong. And Conniff's protestations that his cats were being total dicks did not endear him to anyone, even though scientific study into the nature of house cats has revealed that, yeah, they pretty much are assholes a lot of the time.

Still, everyone assumed Conniff was the bad guy. But it is downright simplistic to call him that, even though, let's face it, he kind of was.

Oh, excuse me, I shouldn't be editorializing. I am supposed to be an impartial reporter of this story. But when you've been covering the domestic pet beat for as long as I have, you can't help but form opinions. For years, I have specialized in reporting on issues involving house cats and their human companions. You might know my byline, Kingsbury Jones, from when I was the chief investigative reporter for *Cat Fancy Magazine*. I also wrote a regular column for *Lonely Shut-In Weekly,* and I was an editor at *Fear of Intimacy Digest.* I know it sounds like I'm bragging about my journalistic career, so in the interest of full disclosure, to show that I'm willing to admit to blots on my resume, I should point out that I also did some writing for *Salon* and *Politico.*

But this case intrigued me more than any other. When I interviewed Conniff, he told me, "I gave my cats food, a roof over their head, and a box to go to the bathroom in, and they repaid me by suing me in a court of law for defamation of character. I still don't get it. I love Millie and Barney."

Conniff's cats, Millie and Barney, were the plaintiffs in this case.

Conniff insists that despite this acrimonious legal battle, he holds no grudge against his cats. "They're adorable," he says. "And as far as their attitude towards me goes, I didn't think they were different from any other cats. I assumed everyone else's cats hated their guts, too. The searing disdain that they showed towards me as I fed them, housed them and scooped up their poop, was just cats being cats, or so I thought. But I guess I was wrong, because instead of thanking me, they got me embroiled in an expensive and time-consuming lawsuit. I can't believe that anyone who spends their time playing with lint and licking their crotches would engage in anything so frivolous."

Conniff has spent a lot of time scooping up after his cats. But this lawsuit was a mess he wasn't going to be able to so easily clean up. To overcome this problem, he would need to employ all his savvy, smarts, and common sense.

In other words, he was screwed.

CHAPTER TWO

The case of Cats v. Conniff was a turning point in the history of American Justice. Never before had house pets sued their owner. For the first time ever, domesticated cats had access to the United States judicial system, and although subsequent research showed that the overwhelming majority of cats in our nation and around the world couldn't care less, this did not make the case any less significant.

It wasn't just cats. Fighting back in the courts had never before been an option for animals of any type. In the past, bears had resolved disputes by clawing humans to death. Pigeons always seemed satisfied with the poetic justice of defecating on people's heads. Cows have long tried to slowly raise people's cholesterol levels over a period of years to the point where humans would keel over and die, but extracting this kind of retribution requires being eaten by people first, and in the long run this might actually be self-defeating.

But never in the annals of law has any animal, much less a house cat, filed suit in an American court of law. In a way it's surprising that this was never done before. One of the great hallmarks of the United States of America is the willingness of its citizens to assert their God-given sense of entitlement. The feeling that we were born great and deserve to have everything handed to us on a silver platter covered with winning lottery tickets is strong in the American spirit. The belief that we deserve everything because of the very fact of our existence is one of the foundations of our modern democracy. So it makes perfect sense that cats would want to get in on this action. For centuries, cats have felt that they had a sense of entitlement coming to them, more so perhaps than any other species. Trust fund frat boys can only dream about being half the spoiled snots that cats are. Even the most privileged moneyed aristocrat has to wipe his own butt. And if there are butlers who perform this service, nobody wants to know about it. But cats have convinced humans to clean up after them, so the next logical step was for cats to have a legal forum to air their grievances.

But in order for the case of Cats v. Conniff to even be considered, a judge had to first be willing to preside over it and many were surprised when Judge Benjamin Lassiter became the man who heard the case.

Known to the legal community as "The Jurisprudent Furry," it is a central part of his legend that he wears a flamboyant dog costume while serving on the bench.

He has made no secret of his predilection for dressing up as a dog and going to Furry conventions, where men and women who enjoy animal cosplay congregate. Judge Lassiter is respected by Furries the world over, and he is not the least bit stung by the criticism he has received from the "Robey" community - the growing group of fetishists who like to organize conventions where they dress in judicial robes. He thinks this is downright weird, but he does not pass judgment on them, even though passing judgment is the very definition of what he does for a living.

The judge's decision to take the Cats v. Conniff case was controversial. There was much talk that a man who dresses up as a dog is not going to treat cats fairly. The attorney for the cats (more on her in a moment) was taken aback by this development. But the judge assured all parties involved that not only did he hold no animosity towards cats, but he was in fact quite fond of them, and had been the owner of several cats himself (until they had all disappeared under mysterious circumstances right around the same time he became known to his friends as a talented gourmet cook of dishes made from exotic meats).

In an interview with this reporter, he stated unequivocally, "Just because I dress as a dog doesn't mean I prefer dogs over cats, it's just that a dog costume happens to be the outfit that I feel most comfortable in, that's all. I tried on a cat costume once and it just seemed undignified to go through the trouble of wearing clothing that provided no erotic satisfaction...we're off the record, right?"

No we weren't off the record, but there was nothing unethical about the judge's stance on cosplay, so he was able to preside over this trial without any further outcry. He had many years as a respected judge under his belt, and even more years of wearing furry dog costumes under, above, and below his belt, so any reasonable person would conclude that he was beyond reproach.

This is what Conniff was up against, but despite the obstacles that lay before him, he had no doubt that taking on the legal system was a task he was more than ready for.

He was very wrong about this. Very, very wrong.

CHAPTER THREE

Not to diminish the contributions of the two cats who filed this lawsuit, but much of the credit for this historic case has to go to their lawyer, Melanie Mason, who initiated the proceedings and brought the case to trial. What's doubly impressive is that she represented Millie and Barney even though she has a severe allergic reaction to cats whenever she is around them.

When not in the vicinity of cats, she is a studious-looking woman in her mid-thirties. She has streaks of grey in her hair and a few wrinkles on her face, but she wears these as a badge of honor that mark the many hours of hard work she's put into a job that she's devoted herself to almost to the exclusion of all else. Her bedraggled appearance would be part of her charm, but charm is not really her thing.

I asked her why she of all people would subject herself to a severe source of physical feline-induced discomfort, and she replied, "Well, I have long been an advocate of animal rights. This has been my specialty as a lawyer. When I'm around cats, I break out into a rash, my skin bloats, and I become a faucet of phlegm, so I feel a connection to them that is more intense than any human connection I've ever had. Cats at least make me feel something."

I asked if she cares about cats more than she cares about people.

"I'd rather not talk about that," she said. "I'm a very private person. And you shouldn't read any psychological implications into this. When I was a child, the only time I received any attention from my parents was when I was physically ill, so I've always been drawn to people who make me sick."

Anticipating my next question, she added, "I've never experienced an allergic reaction to any human, or any other animal, except cats. That's why I like being around them. Their potentially deadly germs make me feel alive."

I was tempted to ask her if she's ever been in therapy, but that's none of my business. So I asked her, "Have you ever been in therapy?"

"That's none of your business," she replied.

Yes, she had been in therapy alright, as have I, and as have just about every person I've ever met. Still, in her case, it seemed that I could use this as a pejorative against her if I ever wanted to smear her on the Internet, but at this point I was leaning towards tilting my reporting in her favor, so I didn't press this line of questioning any further.

Instead, I asked about the challenges of starting a law firm devoted to defending pets.

"Well, although there has been much mistreatment of our animal friends, my law practice has struggled because not many pets are willing to come forward to bring accusations against people. Pets depend on maintaining a level of cuteness and adorability to keep them in the good graces of their so-called human benefactors. Bringing them to court could cause consternation among pet owners. It might make them hesitant to give belly rubs, and worse, the withholding of treats. The last thing an animal who files a lawsuit against a human can expect is a pat on the head."

I pointed out to that most people involved in the cause of animal rights tend to focus on animals abandoned in the street, or endangered species in the wilderness. House pets living in the comfort of a private home are not usually at the top of anyone's list when it comes to animal advocacy.

"I see your point," she said. "But my fighting on behalf of domesticated cats came on the heels of the other causes I took up during my early years as a lawyer - the struggles of affluent millennials living in luxurious homes paid for by their parents, the legal issues faced by television personalities hired solely based on their good looks, the problems of marginally talented pop singers susceptible to faulty auto tune technology. But as compelling as these cases are, I eventually realized that nobody ever thinks about the struggles that your average everyday domestic cat goes through - the meals that appear regularly, the easy access to boxes of kitty litter, the soft piles of laundry that are even more comfortable than the human beds that cats commandeer and claim as their own. No one ever speaks up on behalf of cats who live protected lives in welcoming households. But I decided it was about time somebody did."

This desire on her part might never have been realized, but then she hit upon an issue that she felt was ripe for legal representation.

"The exploitation of domestic house cats on the internet!" she declared, and this indeed was the foundation of the Defamation of Character suit she brought against Conniff on behalf of Millie and Barney.

But first she had to find a way to communicate with cats, and this became a case of Ms. Mason not just overcoming her affliction, but using it to her advantage.

"It's kind of awesome," she said. "I have my allergies to thank for leading me to the breakthrough that enabled me to psychically communicate with cats."

I must admit that at first I was skeptical of this assertion. I thought it was some insane Dr. Doolittle meets Dr. Strange nonsense she was talking about. But this was real. There is indeed a cat food that enables cats to communicate with humans on a scale never before seen. If cats began eating this food on a mass scale it would alter their existence and perhaps cause an evolutionary shift like nothing else in world history. But this did not happen because most of the cats who tried this magical food thought it tasted like crap and refused to take another bite.

But Millie and Barney were willing to eat it, and that is what eventually led to a breakthrough in human/cat communications. It had the potential to change the way people look at animals and transform the way we live in the twenty-first century.

That didn't happen at all, not by a long shot, but it is pertinent to this particular case, so hopefully it was worth mentioning.

CHAPTER FOUR

Ms. Mason knew that if she ever had cat clients, she would need to brace herself for the allergic reaction that was sure to come. "There were many doctor-recommended brands of medication that I could choose from," she said. "But this is the digital age, and I believe in doing things the modern way, so I decided the best course of action would be to search online for something untested that nobody had ever heard of."

So in her quest for cat-related medicine, she happened upon an organic alternative brand called Psychic Diet Cat Food. The makers of this product claimed that if a cat ate this food, he or she would be able to communicate with humans. This seemed far-fetched, especially considering that most humans are barely capable of communicating with each other.

"I ordered a bunch of Psychic Diet Cat Food and put it in the waiting room of my office," Ms. Mason told me, smiling at the memory of the cute ceramic bowl she placed the food in, but wincing as she recalled the lack of foot traffic in her small practice located on the Lower East Side of Manhattan.

The problem for her was that house pets by their very nature never leave their houses, so if you're trying to build up a clientele of cats who never go outside, how are you ever going to attract walk-in business? House cats only leave their homes to go to the veterinarian, and that is almost always under protest.

"But I couldn't let go of my desire to represent the legal interests of house cats, especially after scouring the web and seeing so many instances of cats being photographed and digitally displayed against their wills," she said.

"I saw shocking videos of cats playing pianos, falling into sock drawers, sticking their heads in and out of cardboard boxes, mistaking their own reflections in mirrors, and other humiliating scenarios only meant for the sick amusement of humans."

I pointed out to her that most people find these types of clips delightful and that they are considered an acceptable form of entertainment in polite society. She bristled at the suggestion.

"These are nothing more than snuff films!" she declared.

I was a bit taken aback by this statement, and when I asked what her definition of a snuff film was, she replied that she considered any footage of cats being cutesy, endearing and adorable for the amusement of humans without the written consent of cats is a snuff film. When I pointed out that the traditional definition of a snuff film is a movie that shows a human murdered on camera, she thought about it for a moment and then said, "Yeah, there is a negative aspect to that as well, but what I'm talking about makes human snuff films feel tame by comparison."

There is no doubt that Melanie Mason is an odd woman with provocative ideas, but it takes an unusual person to do something that nobody has ever done before and the case of Cats v. Conniff certainly falls into that category.

And the one thing no one can ever accuse her of is lacking passion. "Who profits from this exploitation of cats?" she asks, her righteous anger spouting forth like Carrie Nation with a severe head cold. "The cats aren't prospering from it, that's for sure! It is only the humans who post this stuff on the Internet for free that make a profit!"

And the more she saw of cat photos and videos on You Tube, Instagram, Facebook and Twitter, the more outraged she became.

"The exploitation of cats in photographs was perhaps even worse than what I was seeing in videos," she said. "I saw pictures of cats with snarky commentary attached, and who were the comments in the comments section addressed to? Not to the cats, but to the posters of the pictures, as if they were the ones who deserve praise for the inherent cuddliness of the cats, not the cuddly cats themselves. So I thought to myself, who will advocate for the adorable? Who will stand up for the helpless kitties whose voices have been neutered?"

I didn't think it was the voices being neutered that bothered the cats so much, but it wasn't my place to debate this with her, so instead I asked Ms. Mason what led her to Millie and Barney.

"Well," she replied. "I decided that if I were to bring these horrible practices to light for the general public, it would be best to file a suit against a celebrity. Unfortunately, that didn't work out, so I had to settle for Frank Conniff."

It was apparent from this statement that she was in danger of underestimating Mr. Conniff. Dismissing an opponent right off the bat is something you do at your own risk. For all she knew, Ms. Mason might very well be up against a formidable adversary and could be in for the fight of her life.

It's a good thing thing she didn't consider any of that because none of it was even remotely true. Turns out her initial underestimation of Conniff was quite accurate.

CHAPTER FIVE

It is true that Mr. Conniff did post several photographs of his cats, Millie and Barney, on Twitter, Instagram, and Facebook.

"As you can see from the pictures, these are adorable cats," Ms. Mason said. "They are living noble lives that should be honored, not ridiculed. But look at some of comments Conniff made to accompany these photos!

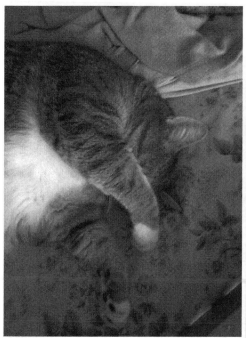

Conniff's comment: "Another productive day for Millie and Barney."
Ms. Mason's response: "At first you think Conniff is paying them a compliment for their work ethic, but then when you see the overall tone of his Twitter feed, you realize he's being sarcastic. The lack of respect is galling!"

Conniff's comment: "Millie and Barney - doing what they do best."

Ms. Mason's response: "This is an example of Conniff being willfully ignorant. Yes, Millie and Barney are masters in the art of slumber. But is it really what they're best at? Their skills at eating, pooping, peeing and staring off into space are just as impressive, which is why this tweet can only be interpreted as passive-aggressive at best."

Conniff's comment: "Millie and Barney, showing their devotion and deep interest in me."

Ms. Mason's response: "With Conniff, it's always about him, isn't it? He seems to me like the kind of egomaniac that would write about himself in the third person. Millie and Barney don't bug him when he's binge-watching Netflix, so he shouldn't complain about them when they binge-watch the wall."

Conniff's comment: "Millie in a state of jubilant celebration when I come home."

Ms. Mason's response: "For heaven's sake, what does Conniff want? She's taking time out from a nap to look up and stare at him! She acknowledging his existence, and all he can do is make fun of her. What a jerk!"

Conniff's comment: "The most important part of any major project is teamwork."

Ms. Mason's response: "This statement is true enough, but it doesn't apply to this particular situation. Conniff was too dim to know that at this moment, Millie and Barney had two completely different agendas, and just happened to be on the same bed as they pursued their separate goals."

Conniff's comment: "Millie and Barney reveling in the passing parade of life."

Ms. Mason's response: "Since Conniff rarely gets off his ass to do anything, what they are watching is the crappiest parade of all time, so Conniff should be expressing sympathy, not snark."

Conniff's comment: "Millie is sitting on a different suitcase! This is a game changer!"

Ms. Mason's response: "Rather than praise Millie for having a willingness to change and grow, Conniff ridicules her, perhaps because a middle aged man with a Darth Vader action figure doesn't want to confront his own stillborn maturity."

CHAPTER SIX

There was visible anger in Ms. Mason's face even though it was mostly covered with bandages.

"As you can see, Mr. Conniff was not content to merely post the pictures of his cats and let the images speak for themselves," she said. "No, he had to insert his own snarky, belittling commentary to go along with the photos. I was sure that if his cats saw this, their feelings would be hurt."

"And you thought Millie and Barney had a legal recourse?" I asked.

"Yes!" she said. "Conniff's internet postings of his cat photos were as clear a case of defamation of character as I have ever seen. And my suspicions were later confirmed when I found out that these disparaging tweets were being posted without the knowledge or approval of Millie or Barney. Conniff was exploiting his cats for his own personal amusement and for the cheap entertainment of his followers on social media."

I asked her what she had against people being amused.

"Nothing!" she replied. "Look, I admit, I have no sense of humor. So you would think that I'd be the ideal audience for Mr. Conniff's stand-up comedy. I am a stoic person, but I also know that when it comes to dour negativity, it takes a village. I dream of a world where I can share my humorlessness with everyone, and my inability to laugh is infectious. But that is still just a utopian dream. So in the meantime I wanted to help these cats find justice."

What she was saying came from a place of passion and possibly psychosis. But she was also practical, and she knew that Millie and Barney were house pets who never left their apartment, so getting them to agree to sue

Conniff and hire her as their lawyer would be a challenge, and it would require every bit of ingenuity she had.

But actually, the whole thing turned out to be an easy, routine task that she could have just phoned in. The path before her held no twists, turns, or surprises, but the author would consider it a personal favor if you kept reading anyway.

CHAPTER SEVEN

Ms. Mason got the idea that a way to reach Mr. Conniff's cats might be through the medium of the internet. The source of their defamation would also be the source of their salvation, or so she hoped. She would send a subliminal message to them by way of whatever kind of Internet content Conniff would in all likelihood be watching. But what kind of programing might that be?

"Porn," Ms. Mason decided. "The obvious answer was porn."

The plan was for her to insert an advertisement directed at the the cats into whatever porn site Conniff might be watching, and his cats would see it if they happened to be looking over his shoulder during the two or three hours of the day they were awake during the five or six hours a day that Conniff was watching porn.

But Ms. Mason had to surmise which porn sites Mr. Conniff favored. Once again, her lawyerly talent for deduction came into play.

"I saw on his Facebook page that Conniff described himself as 'Writer. Comedian. Gout Sufferer.' The writer and comedian part I found hard to believe, but judging by his aged appearance, gout sufferer was certainly plausible."

So she checked out some of the more popular gout-themed porn sites:

Barely Feeble (young women in the early stages of gout).

Arthritis Mingle (mainly a dating site, even though no one had ever hooked up on it because no one in its target audience was capable of swiping right).

Girls Gone Gimpy.

"This last one seemed the most perverted, so I assumed it would be the one Mr. Conniff would most likely frequent," Ms. Mason said.

This assumption proved to be correct.

"I paid for an ad to air right in the middle of a scene with a woman wearing nothing more than a three piece business suit while she rubbed her ankle in pain. If that wasn't sick enough, the 'money shot' was a close-up of her being prescribed anti-inflammatory medication by a rheumatologist."

Ms. Mason still seemed traumatized by the memory of watching this depraved scenario. It was obvious to any observer that she was a woman who had had little exposure to pornographic materials. But she bravely continued to describe more of the disturbing images she had witnessed.

"On the heels of this, there was a long sequence accompanied by funky wha-wha pedal guitar music, with explicit footage of a woman signing insurance forms, and believe me, you could see *everything*. It was so demented I could barely look, but the well-being of two cats was at stake, so I didn't avert my eyes."

Those eyes filled with tears as she recalled the uric-acid-based perversions she had witnessed, but she told herself it was all worth it, and at least she had not suffered this trauma in vain.

But alas it was in vain; it ultimately had nothing to do with how she eventually became Millie and Barney's lawyer. She was emotionally scarred for life, all for nothing. But she was still determined to be a permanently scarred person who won an important court case, and it is a tribute to her fortitude that she did not give up.

CHAPTER EIGHT

The eventual meeting between Melanie Mason and Millie and Barney came about through an unusual alignment of technology and luck.

"Since the porn thing didn't work out, I figured the only way a cat would contact me would be if they randomly typed in words on a computer keyboard, and that happened to be a website I set up," Ms Mason said. "So I registered the domain name, www.pqksdjfhqshkfkhjnmdsncsknpwdpkjn.com." It was my hope that the words I had randomly chosen would also be the words that a cat would randomly and obliviously type. It was a long shot, but it just might work."

It didn't.

CHAPTER NINE

"I abandoned my initial plan and came up with a new idea," Ms. Mason said. " I decided the only thing to do was sneak into Mr. Conniff's apartment under false pretenses."

A bold move to be sure, and I asked her if she had any misgivings about the ethics of such a legally dubious action.

She thought long and hard about this for a moment, then replied, "No."

But still, this was a tricky proposition. Ms. Mason was clearly outside of her comfort zone. A shy woman by nature, entering the lobby of Conniff's building and approaching the doorman would require a social aggressiveness she had never previously shown. And yet she would have to be subtle, not draw attention to herself, or raise suspicions. Above all she had to give the impression that nothing out of the ordinary was taking place.

"I'm here to have sex with Mr. Conniff in exchange for money," she said to the doorman of Conniff's building. The doorman handed her a key with the bored indifference of an assembly line worker doing a mundane task he had done a million times before. She was let right up.

Ms. Mason knocked on Conniff's door a couple times, and when there was no response, she turned the lock and entered the apartment. As luck would have it, Conniff was not home.

The first thing Ms. Mason had to deal with was the stark, barren, post-apocalyptic landscape of Mr. Conniff's abode. "A futon, a chair, bookshelves, a table with a TV, and cat hair floating in the air like tired locus," was how she described the setting . "The cat hair was sending my allergies into Def Con 4 mode, but the sound of me pouring Psychic Diet cat food into the food dish sent Barney scurrying out from wherever he was hiding. Millie stayed concealed underneath the futon and I could hear her hissing at me, but I knew this was some sort of post-traumatic stress disorder affliction from her time with Mr. Conniff."

Eventually, the smell of new cat food lured Millie out of hiding and she and Barney reacted enthusiastically to the food. Although Psychic Diet cat food is to this day an unpopular brand with most cats, Millie and Barney considered it a gourmet meal compared to the substandard fare they had come to expect from Mr. Conniff. (And for the record, that brand is no longer being marketed. Despite its bargain price, Arby's Cat Food never really caught on, even though several consumer organizations said that it tasted better than regular Arby's.)

"Look," Ms. Mason told me. "My expectations were realistic. I assumed the Psychic Diet cat food would enable Millie and Barney to start psychically communicating with me, nothing more. But what happened next was beyond anything I ever could have imagined."

Ms. Mason endured a severe allergic reaction as she waited for the cats to give her a deposition. But to her surprise, Barney coughed up a statement as soon as he finished eating his new cat food. Or, to be more accurate, he puked up his statement.

It should be noted here that Psychic Diet cat food is alphabet shaped. So when Barney started throwing up his food, instead of a formless glop of gloop, he up-chucked fully formed words, sentences, and paragraphs. Whatever else you wanted to say about Barney, there was no denying that he expressed himself very elegantly through his vomit.

Here is what Barney said:

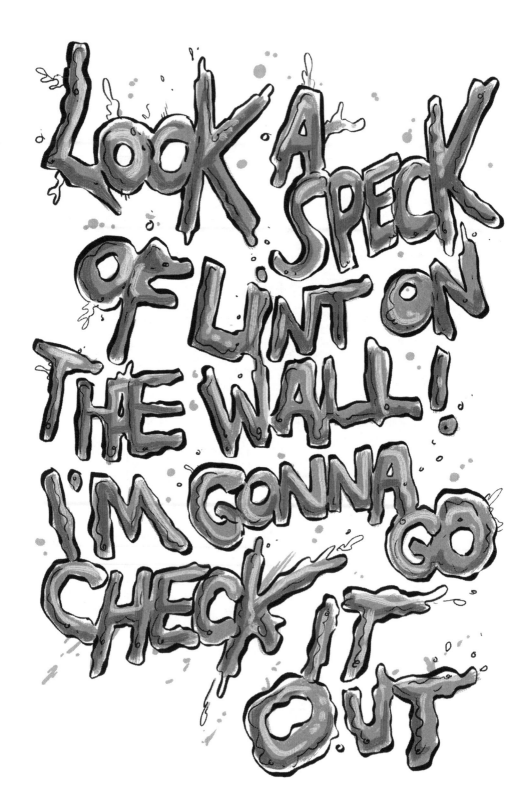

It wasn't long before Millie started throwing up her own words on the floor as well, and her testimony was even more opinionated than Barney's:

THAT SPECK OF LINT IS OVERRATED I LOOKED AT IT FOR SIX HOURS YESTERDAY BEFORE I GOT BORED AND WENT BACK TO SLEEP

Now that Ms. Mason knew she could communicate with Millie and Barney, she was confident she could extract damning testimony from them against Mr. Conniff. There was now no looking back, and not just because her eyes were so swollen from her allergies that she could barely see anything.

Ms. Mason's ability to do her job regardless of physical adversity is certainly an inspirational tale. As she patiently sat and translated Millie and Barney's scribbled vomit into words on paper, she endured violent sneezing spasms because she knew that every piece of snot that flew out of her nose was a booger on behalf of justice.

CHAPTER TEN

In building Millie and Barney's defamation case against Mr. Conniff, Ms. Mason had a large trove of documentation to work with. Over the course of several years, on Facebook, Twitter, Instagram and You Tube, Mr. Conniff had made many disparaging and hurtful remarks about Millie and Barney. But these facts alone were not what outraged Ms. Mason.

"What really upset me was that he was exploiting Millie and Barney to build up his presence and gain more followers on social media," she said. "The inherent adorableness of these two cats was apparent to everyone. If you look at the comments on Twitter and Facebook, there are many posts along the lines of, 'Aw!' and 'too cute!'"

This is not an exaggeration. Many internet users did indeed come to the conclusion that these cats were not just cute, but were in fact, "too cute."

"Anyone who posted pictures of these beauties was sure to gain a huge social media following," Ms. Mason said. "And yet Mr. Conniff not only exploited his pets, but he was so threatened by their popularity that he couldn't help but passive-aggressively lash out at them. This had to stop! And now that I had filed a brief on behalf of Millie and Barney, all I had to do was wait for the go-ahead to take Frank Conniff to court. Unfortunately, what should have been one of the greatest moments of my life was ruined because thanks to an adverse side-effect of my medication, I went into anaphylactic shock and was in a coma when the news came that the trial was going forward."

But due to an inner strength that cannot be measured by mere medical practice, she regained consciousness, and was able to be there for her clients. And Ms. Mason had no doubt that those clients, Millie and Barney, were as hungry for justice as she was.

Actually, what they were hungry for was tuna fish. But regardless of who was hungry for what, the trial began not long after Ms. Mason came out of her coma. It was expected that Mr. Conniff would seek high-powered representation to defend him against these charges, but much to everyone's surprise, he decided to serve as his own attorney during the proceedings.

You could say that the legal community had differing opinions about this strategy, if by "differing opinions," you mean that the overall consensus was that it was an act of sheer idiocy on Conniff's part.

But Mr. Conniff gave a different, more nuanced reason for his actions.

"Going to trial is expensive," he told me. "And say what you will about my legal skills, but I am a super cheap lawyer, the kind you'd find at the Dollar Store."

I asked if he fancied himself an ambulance chaser.

"No, my chronic flareups of gout rule out chasing anything of any kind."

Fair enough. He had no experience in this field so he cut a reasonable deal with himself. And when I interviewed him, he was adamant about his innocence and the unfairness of Millie and Barney's charges against him.

"I love my cats, I'm very tolerant of many of their quirks and foibles, but they were really out of line when they took me to court," he said.

I asked him if he denied that he exploited and insulted them on social media.

"Of course I deny it!" he replied. "Look, it's true that I do have a somewhat sizable following on social media, but except for the hundreds upon hundreds of retweets and new followers I get whenever I post pictures of them, my cats have had a minimal impact on that following. Maybe that's why they hate my guts. And just to be clear, when Barney bites me, and I scream, 'I'm going to kill you' at the top of my lungs, I mean it in an affectionate way."

I stopped Mr. Conniff right there. I asked him if he really had threatened his cats with death.

"No, of course not!" he protested. "In the heat of the moment, I may have sometimes threatened to kill them, but that should in no way be misinterpreted as a death threat," he said, oblivious to the hole he was digging for himself.

"What about the many times you've gone on record saying to your cats, 'I'm going to freaking kill you, you little bastards'? I asked, citing a transcript from a deposition one of his neighbors gave.

"I tend to say things like that after Millie decides to treat my brand new sneakers as a cauldron for her cat pee, or after Barney has been sitting peacefully on my lap and an unexpected noise causes him to use his claws to go all Lizzie Borden on my leg. But look, my cats, for all their faults, are wonderful little creatures. I just love having them around, to pet and cuddle, and hold in my arms, until for no reason out of the blue they scratch and wound me unprovoked *AND THE I JUST WANT TO STRANGLE THE LITTLE BUGGERS UNTIL THEY...*"

At this point Mr. Conniff stopped what he was saying and became self-conscious.

"Uh, can we go off the record now?" he asked.

I obliged him, and everything he said for the rest of this particular interview was off the record, which is weird, because he then spent the next three hours expressing innocuous, uncontroversial opinions about *Star Wars: The Force Awakens.*

Conniff didn't want to admit it, but the threat of this trial was highly stressful to him. He was the in over his head, that much was clear. But it is not the place of this reporter to judge this man's actions, or to take sides, even if it was obvious in no uncertain terms that he deserved to lose the case.

CHAPTER ELEVEN

In response to a request from Mr. Conniff, who is concerned about the financial consequences of this lawsuit from his cats, there will be no chapter eleven in this book. It is a stupid request, and honoring it had no effect whatsoever on the outcome of the case, but it was honored nonetheless because as William Shakespeare once wrote, "The quality of mercy is not strained...something, something...whatever."

CHAPTER TWELVE

Now that we are no longer in Chapter Eleven, we can discuss the damages that Conniff's cats sued him for:

The first part of their defamation of character suit was a demand for $1 million worth of chicken, beef and fish-flavored wet cat food.

The one million dollars alone was more than Mr. Conniff could afford, but the settlement stipulated that if the cats became bored with the food, they had the option of rejecting it, and then Conniff would be obligated to buy them a million dollars worth of whatever other cat food catered to their whims at that particular moment. Legal analysts estimated that based on the unpredictable behavior of cats in general, the cost to Conniff could well have reached well into the billions of dollars. Of course there was no way he could ever pay this, but a judgment of this sort against Conniff would tie up whatever assets he possessed and more or less ruin his life forever.

The cats could never put a price on how awesome this would make them feel.

Millie and Barney also demanded a Furniture Warehouse.

That's right, the cats stipulated that Conniff buy a furniture warehouse filled with merchandise that they could scratch at will.

But this request, in the unlikely event that it was fulfilled, would in all likelihood hit a snag when the zoning commission inevitably ruled that for a cat, a warehouse filled not just with furniture, but also upholstery, drapes and curtains, is like an amusement park, and getting permits for a theme park in a warehouse district is all but impossible.

The cats then threw a curve ball of yarn by demanding as part of their settlement the head of Andrew Lloyd Webber.

For some, this was a controversial stipulation. Millie and Barney's distaste for the musical "Cats" led them to the idea that they would not have satisfaction until they could see the be-knighted British composer's severed head on a spit. Many were shocked by this request, and yet it was ultimately the most quickly approved of all the items on their agenda.

These were major damages that Millie and Barney called for, but the one that meant the most to them was their demand that they henceforth be referred to by their actual, real names.

Their real names? According to Millie and Barney, cats are born with monikers that are bestowed upon them by ancient ancestors. Some have called this the most startling revelation to emerge from the case, and if that's true then God help us, because that means this case isn't all that particularly interesting.

CHAPTER THIRTEEN

Overcome by a bout of superstition due to what he considers to be a wave of bad luck, Mr. Conniff has requested that there not be a chapter thirteen in this book. In normal circumstances, this request would be ignored, but as it happens, this volume is being edited during National Placate A Moron Week, so his request will be honored, which ironically enough, is a stroke of good luck for him.

CHAPTER FOURTEEN

According to Millie and Barney, they, like all cats, have to suffer through the insipid names they are given by humans, names like, well, Millie and Barney.

If we are to believe Barney, his name is actually His Majesty, the Earl of Awesome. While it might seem unlikely to our human sensibilities that an ancient animal would bestow the name of His Majesty, the Earl of Awesome on a descendant, Barney (as he is commonly known) insists that this is exactly what happened.

Millie claims that her real name is Goddess Of Blood, a reference no doubt to her propensity for using her claws to extract blood from any humans who dare try to pick her up, or -- even more egregious as far as she's concerned -- dare look at her for any extended period of time. While it does not seem plausible that this name is her spiritual birthright, a panel of historical linguists did conclude that it is, in their summation, "a pretty friggin' cool name."

Raising the issue of proper naming was seen by some as a needless distraction from the main thrust of this case, and calling them by the names they insisted on was not deemed their legal right by the judge, but their ability to even enter it into the record was seen by many as a setback for Mr. Conniff, and more importantly, the notion that cats could have a legal right to deciding what they are named was an issue that could potentially impact cats and their owners in a profound and lasting way.

But that didn't happen, so in retrospect I guess I'm sorry that I brought it up.

CHAPTER FIFTEEN

Before the start of the trial, this reporter had a conversation with Conniff in which he tried to put a positive spin on what the world was now seeing as a contentious relationship with his cats.

"Look, no matter what I do on their behalf, Barney treats me with contempt, and Millie hisses at me for the simple crime of arriving home," Conniff stated. "I know that this is because they only see me as a cat food delivery system and an on-call belly rubbing and poop cleaning service. They don't seem to understand why I persist in hanging around the apartment long after I've performed my feeding and scooping duties. But I still can't help but look at my cats with fondness, even though my looking at them with fondness always seems to inspire them to look back at me with searing, insatiable hatred. But, other than that, I think we get along just fine."

Mr. Conniff didn't seem to realize that explaining his motivation for posting snarky comments about his cats on Facebook, Twitter and Instagram was not endearing him to anyone. In recent years, social media has come into its own as an effective forum for such productive activities as making unfounded accusations against other human beings and participating in vicious pile-ons when celebrities engage in despicable, immoral behavior, like gaining a few pounds or wearing a dress that's different from the dress you thought they should wear to a red carpet event. In some instances, Twitter and Facebook are effective vehicles for pointing out the moral failings of people whose faces change as they get older, or better still, expressing umbrage when a comedian does a joke that is offensive to the delicate sensibilities of schoolmarmish bloggers. But when a comedian such as Mr. Conniff abuses his computer privileges with humorous disparagement of his cats, you can expect a backlash. The wages of whimsey are high in 21st century America. This is why Conniff soon found himself in a courtroom facing a furry judge, a prosecuting attorney heavily under the influence of prescription medication, and two cats that he once considered friends but were now his opponents in the eyes of the law.

Conniff had once thought the main advantage of being a cat owner was that they were a cinch to take care of. Normal domestic house cats are indeed relatively easy to manage. But as Conniff soon found out, when your normal domestic house cats have legal representation, you probably would have been much better off owning a turtle.

CHAPTER SIXTEEN

The day of the trial arrived. Conniff entered the court carrying his cats in two separate carrying cases. They expressed their displeasure with piercing yowls of anguished complaint that made all the spectators in the room feel that they were witnesses to a tragedy, even though Millie and Barney made the exact same noise when a can of food was being opened, or when they happened to see a bird fly by their apartment window, or when either of them was bored in the middle of the afternoon and felt like making an annoying sound for no reason.

Conniff tried to explain this to anyone who would listen, but no one would listen. Everybody in the room was looking at him like he had just ordered the Death Star to blow up PETA headquarters, so he opened the cat carriers as soon as he sat at his table and Mille and Barney were free to roam as they pleased, but being that they were apartment cats, roaming as they pleased was not something they were used to.

But Ms. Morgan had cleverly placed kitty litter under her table and cat food on top of it, so the two cats immediately ran over to where she was. This was the side of the courtroom the cats were supposed to be on during the trial, but in the preceding weeks, Millie and Barney had continued living with Conniff because they were still legally obliged to do so.

The atmosphere in that apartment had been rife with tension. The two cats refused to look at Conniff, they showed no appreciation of anything he did, and if they interacted with him at all, it was to snarl and snap at him. So Mr. Conniff was relived that despite the litigious situation with his pets, at least things were still normal around the house.

The courtroom gallery was filled with people from all walks of life - stoned millennial dudes taking a break from Improv Traffic Court, stylish young women who aspired to one day be crazy cat ladies, earnest law students anxious to witness American judicial history, amateur philosophers seeking to understand the true meaning of pointlessness, and animal rights activists questioning their life choices. Plus, the Frank Conniff Fan Club was represented in full force, although after a few minutes that guy left and went home.

The room quieted down as the bailiff stepped before the judge's bench and faced the crowd. He had a stiff, smooth face that was as God made it, yet seemed to be the product of plastic surgery. His tanning salon skin and full head of toupee blended perfectly with the officers uniform he wore, a real and official get-up that somehow had less gravitas than a valet parking attendant's outfit. He was in his forties, with the false bravado of a man half his age.

It quickly became clear that whatever skills he had as a court officer were secondary to his talent for audience warmup:

"Ladies and gentleman, are you ready to get all judicial?" he asked in a cadence that was definitely not his indoor voice.

There was a minor round of applause, so he repeated himself:

"I said, are you ready for some litigation?"

This time he got a bigger reaction but not enough to satisfy him:

"*I CAN'T HEAR YOU!*"

This was not true; he could hear them, but he wasn't under oath, and this time the assembled onlookers clapped to his satisfaction, so he finally got to the main point he was trying to make:

"All rise for the honorable Judge Benjamin Lassiter."

The judge entered the courtroom in full furry canine regalia, but Millie and Barney barely looked up and took notice of him. Everyone else in the courtroom rose.

Ms. Mason stood by the cat's table. Much of her face was bloated and covered in gauze, but she was fully prepared to make an impassioned case on behalf of Millie and Barney. And if she had any concern over the cats not showing respect for the judge, she had confidence that the judge would not take it personally and factor in that they were cats and thus had no respect for anyone or anything that they couldn't eat, scratch or defecate on.

So the trial began and nobody knew what to expect. So many modern issues were stirred into the meow mix of this trial - cat ownership, human responsibility, social media, and the codes and behaviors that navigate us through the digital age.

If Millie and Barney had ever been aloof and indifferent, the time had come for them to change their attitudes and engage in the world around them. The stakes couldn't be higher.

But they were splayed out on the table, sound asleep. They really didn't give a shit.

CHAPTER SEVENTEEN

Conniff stepped up to make his opening statement. Many had thought that he was foolish to represent himself in this case, and he was out to prove them wrong.

He didn't.

"Ms. Mason has spent a lot of time criticizing me for posting pictures of my cats on the internet," Conniff began. "But, in fact, that's exactly the kind of thing our Founding Fathers had in mind when they founded our great nation!"

The judge raised his eyes in skepticism, which caused the furry eyebrows pasted on his forehead to arch upwards, and a murmur that sounded like a Gregorian chant of "huh?" went up in the room, but Conniff continued:

"The founders of our county knew that Americans ravaged by war would want something adorable to look at to soothe their weary souls. Since the technology for photographs wasn't available back then, citizens would go to the town square and hold up their cats so passing pedestrians could look at them and say, 'aw, too cute!' just like the way modern citizens do when they're scrolling through the internet eight hours a day. But back then, in the open space of the town square, those beautifully adorable kitties gave our young nation a sense of what freedom was all about. Plus it was fun for women and children to pet the cats while the men went about the business of buying and selling slaves."

At this point the court stenographer threw her dictation device at Conniff, hitting him on the side of the head and knocking him to the floor. Not a single person in the courtroom, including the judge, thought this was a wrong thing to do.

Conniff rose back to his feet, rubbing his bruised head in pain. He looked over at the stenographer. She was a studious-looking woman with bad posture and good bone structure. She was in her early forties, which for Conniff would have been robbing the cradle, but he later told this reporter he was smitten.

"She threw a heavy metallic object at the side of my head," he said. "I wanted to go over and ask if she was coming on to me, but I was afraid the stroll across the room would make me pass out."

So Conniff stayed on his side of the court and continued his opening statement, stubbornly devoted to his inane line of reasoning:

"Of course, town square cat selfies were a challenge during colonial times and before the age of photography. It wasn't until Mathew Brady came along during the Civil War that cat photography became a viable practice; however, Mr. Brady became so annoyed by the aloof and indifferent attitudes of the cats he was trying to photograph that he began taking Civil War photos as a way to calm down after the stress of being around cats."

"Objection!"

This word rang throughout the court room. It was only after a moment that people realized it was the judge saying it.

"That's the stupidest thing I've ever heard," the judge said. "I ask that Mr. Conniff's statement be stricken from the record! Approved!"

The fact that the judge was agreeing with himself so readily was an indication that the trial was already not going well for Conniff.

Ms. Mason then stood before the judge, transmitting a confidence that was a stark contrast to Mr. Conniff's presentation, which had the awkward vibe of an untalented novice doing his first open mic.

"This is a total fabrication on the part of Mr. Conniff, a complete misreading of American History," Ms Morgan stated. "Cats formed no alliances during the Civil War. They were indifferent to the issue of who should win, the North or the South. And unlike humans, cats were not racists during this conflict. In truth, whenever you see a cat showing disdain for any human being, it is not because they are prejudiced. It is because they are firm believers in States' Rights."

An argument could have been made against the historical accuracy of this remark, but the judge nodded his head in agreement and said "overruled!" before Mr. Conniff even had the chance to say, "objection," which he wouldn't have said anyway, considering that he had buried in face his hands and was softly sobbing.

Emboldened by the judge's not so subtle encouragement, Ms. Mason enthusiastically continued on:

"But we are getting away from the topic at hand, which is Mr. Conniff's disparagement of Millie and Barney on social media. His cats, in turn, did not make a habit of disparaging his work online or in any other forum. For one thing, they are not particularly familiar with what he has referred to as his, uh, 'comedy'...'"

It should be noted for the record that every person in the courtroom, with the exception of Mr. Conniff, simultaneously made the "air quote" gesture with their fingers as Ms. Mason said the word "comedy."

"These cats don't know anything about his stand up routine," she continued, "because -- and this will surprise no one -- during this century he has rarely been on TV, and as house cats, that's the only way they could possibly see him in action."

"That's not true!" Conniff said. "I taped a performance I did at the Creek and the Cave comedy club in Long Island City..."

"Ooh, Long Island City!" the judge interrupted, the tone of mockery in his voice dripping like battery acid. *The Big Time!*"

Everyone in the room laughed, even Ms. Mason, who's easy out-of-the-gate success in the trial seemed to be awakening a sense of humor she never knew she had.

But Conniff was not laughing. He seemed to take umbrage that anyone would disparage a stand-up set he did on a Tuesday night in front of eight people in a club it took him two different subway lines to get to.

"Your Honor," Conniff said. "The point is that Millie and Barney have seen my stand up comedy. They were with me when I watched and reviewed that tape in my apartment."

"And what did they think?" Ms. Mason asked. Her demeanor suggested that she was expecting a punch line to a joke that Conniff would be the butt of. She was not wrong.

"Uh, my cats," Conniff said. "They gave me good feedback."

"How so?"

"They, uh, they slept through my routine, which was good feedback because it meant I needed to punch up my act."

"So your cats haven't seen your stand-up act after all," Ms. Mason said. "But Millie and Barney have seen your tweets, and like a majority of Americans, they don't think they're the least bit funny, mainly because of the political content, which they find arch and pedantic."

"Objection!" Conniff yelled, maybe to the judge, but more likely to voices in his own head. "My political tweets are a whole different issue from my cat tweets. That last statement should be inadmissible."

The judge stated quizzically at Conniff. "Who are you again?" he said, squinting his eyes.

"I'm the defendant in this trial!" Conniff replied, with an indignation that seemed to come easily to him.

"Oh, right, right," the judge said, his face grimacing as if a repressed memory had just returned to him. "Okay, sustained. Whatever. Why not?"

The judge's decision may have seemed haphazard, but leaving politics out of this equation was a wise move. Millie and Barney are not affiliated with any political party; like most cats, they see themselves as Independents. But they tend to lean towards a conservative point of view. Like many house cats, they are opposed to any kind of change at all. A new set of furniture or a piece a luggage being moved or a rearrangement of any design element in an apartment tends to make them nostalgic for a moment or two earlier in their lives when the furniture was in the place it was originally supposed to be. It's not uncommon for cats to wistfully look back on that time in their lives when the bookshelf leaned against the right wall of the apartment and not the left wall, when the laundry basket was easily accessible for naps before radical ideas became the vogue and a lidded hamper was suddenly the new normal. Any expert on animal behavior will tell you that when it comes to the human landlords who legislate their lives, most cats prefer limited oversight and intervention.

Ms. Mason did not retreat from addressing these and other issues. The trial was just getting started, and some observes were heard to say that this was going to be the most important legal proceeding since the Scopes Monkey Trial.

Those observers were wrong, this trial didn't have anything like the historical import of that case, but hopefully you'll continue reading anyway.

CHAPTER EIGHTEEN

"Look," Ms. Mason said, addressing the judge and an increasingly exhausted-looking Conniff. "I won't deny that at certain points, Millie and Barney have treated Mr. Conniff as a scratching post..."

The judge interrupted this with a boisterous laugh. "I'm sorry," he said when he finally regained his composure. "But that is a funny image."

Conniff stood up. "Your Honor," he said. "Seems like you've got a great sense of humor. I've got a new CD of my stand up comedy, which is available at..."

"Sit down!" the judge snapped. "This court will not tolerate any attempts by you to market yourself."

"If it please the court, I'd like to establish my brand."

"Shut up and sit down!"

Mr. Conniff did as he was told and Mason resumed:

"The point I was making is that these cats never, ever make fun of Conniff's work. But he, on the other hand, disparages their work all the time."

"What work?" Conniff demanded, rising to his feet like a sleeping vagrant roused into consciousness by a billy club. "What exactly is it that Millie and Barney do for a living?"

Conniff stared at his cats as he said this, but Millie was staring at something that has yet to be determined at press time, and Barney was sprawled out on the table, fast asleep, yet even with his eyes closed, he still had a palpable look of contempt on his face.

Ms. Mason faced the room and held up a ledger book for all to see.

"What I am holding here is Millie and Barney's work schedule."

"I didn't know they kept a Daily Planner," Conniff said.

"There's a lot about your cats you don't know," Ms. Mason said. "Based on psychic interviews I've had with them, I've transcribed Millie and Barney's work schedule into something I like to call... Millie and Barney's work schedule."

She then read from the book:

"10AM -- Arise mid-morning to give ourselves some time to get our chores done before Mr. Waste of Space awakens."

She turned to the judge, and almost as an aside said, "That's the nickname they've given to Conniff."

Mrs. Mason and the judge snickered conspiratorially, then she returned to reading from the book:

"We have breakfast, eating the same crappy Arby's cat food that Mr. Waste of Space supplies to us for lunch, dinner, and between meal snacks. We immediately repurpose this food through our digestive tracts and give it a second life in the cat litter box. We sit and admire our creation for a few moments. As busy as we are, sometimes you just have to stop and smell the feces."

"10:15 -- The entire process of waking up, eating, peeing and crapping has been an emotional roller coaster ride, so we go back to sleep."

"12 Noon -- The inevitable annoyance: Mr. Waste of Space awakens. We always hope that somehow this won't happen. Not that we wish him harm, but it would be a lovely development if he stopped breathing. We realize this is an impractical stance to take, but his irritating insistence on using up oxygen is something we've never gotten used to."

"12:05 - He aimlessly wanders to and from the bathroom, eventually settling in on his aptly named Lazy-boy chair. This is a piece of furniture

that we have performed endless improvements upon, using our claws as a means of self-expression, turning a boring surface into an innovative labyrinth of vandalism-based art, yet Mr. Waste of Space has never expressed a moment of appreciation to us for our work. On the contrary, he disparages us and exults in his own ignorance."

"1:15PM -- He has spent the last hour or so watching TV, surfing the Internet, listening to music (mostly jazz, we hate jazz!), never once taking into consideration that he's disturbing our carefully planned workday. If we don't get the proper amount of sleep in the afternoon, it might very well leave us too tired to get the sleep we need in the evening. The truth is, we are so dedicated to what we do, we often put in double shifts, but Mr. Waste of Space has no appreciation for how hard we toil at our craft."

"3:30PM -- Despite everything, we muster our deep reserves of professionalism and manage to achieve a deep sleep. We are in that sweet spot when our paws are covering our eyes and we have achieved the maximum adorableness that inspires humans to do our bidding. And this is the exact moment Waste of Space photographs us and posts our pictures on the Internet, accompanied by his snarky, hurtful remarks. It is as if all the hours of work we put in is just to provide him with a subject of ridicule, and the kindness we show by allowing him the privilege of feeding us and housing and cleaning up our turds ultimately weans nothing. This would really hurt our feelings if we gave a damn, but we don't. Still, that doesn't make any of this right."

"6:00PM -- After Conniff takes a dump, the magnitude of which is worthy of a visit from FEMA, and makes us wish they manufactured hazmat suits for cats, he bathes (just barely) and dresses (incompetently) and finally leaves the house to do whatever it is he does. We take this opportunity to get some genuinely restful sleep to prepare us for the slightly less restful sleep we'll get later when he comes home."

Ms. Mason put down the book she had been reading and let the gravity of it all sink in with the Judge and the courtroom spectators. Conniff, unable to contain his exasperation, reverted to his go-to default sarcasm. As was often the case during this trial, he made a miscalculation.

"Are you done?" he said, his voice dripping with a venom that was meant to be lethal but didn't even have the kick of a children's vitamin.

"Oh, I'm just getting started," Mason replied.

The spectators applauded and the judge stepped down from the bench and high-fived her, an act which some interpreted as partiality on his part, but which he later insisted was just his individualistic way of saying order in the court.

Whatever the virtues of this judge, any impartial observer could see that he was blatantly partial. Conniff now had a legitimate grievance that at the very least could lead to a mistrial and on the other extreme the disbarment of the judge. It was a path to victory that even an inexperienced lawyer like Conniff could not easily pass up.

But Conniff did pass it up. His entire preparation for the case consisted of him watching old episodes of *Owen Marshall: Counsellor at Law* and *Judd For The Defense*, two television shows from a half century ago that are so obscure, all of their plot lines are inadmissible in a court of modern law. In other words, Conniff didn't know what the hell he was doing, so the trial continued on as before.

CHAPTER NINETEEN

After Ms. Mason and the judge had finished sharing a private joke, the judge went back to the bench and Ms. Mason resumed her tirade against Conniff.

"I would now like to point out another area of grievance on the part of Millie and Barney," she said. "I'm talking about the fact that Mr. Conniff has subjected them to many defective so-called 'cat toys.'"

"What does that have to do with defamation of character?" Conniff protested.

"I'll tell you what that has to do with it," the judge said. "Shut up! That's what it has to do with it!"

Now that this point of order was settled, Ms. Mason continued. She held up a battered looking toy rubber mouse.

"Conniff tried to pass this off to his cats as a 'mouse.' Now, based on their natural instincts, any cat would find a mouse to be an enjoyable toy. The fun comes from chasing them around the house, catching them, and then biting into their flesh until they let out a high-pitched squeal that indicates they are in a state of unbearable pain and overwhelming terror as the mouse's intestines come pouring out like a can of spaghettiOs."

"For a so-called animal lover, you certainly have a cavalier attitude towards mice," Conniff interjected.

"Okay, quick survey," an unfazed Ms. Mason said in immediate response. "Who in this courtroom is an animal lover?"

Everyone raised their hands, except Millie and Barney, but since they were cats, their high self-regard went without question.

Ms. Mason then added, "And who here hates rodents?"

Everyone raised their hands once again.

She then looked at Conniff and said, "I might remind you that the test of a first rate intelligence is the ability to hold two opposing ideas in mind at the same time and still retain the ability to function. Would you agree, Mr. Conniff?"

Conniff did not respond, because his brain was so overtaxed all he could do was twitch and drool. It was quite obvious that no matter how many opposing ideas were in his head, he hadn't the foggiest notion what any of them meant.

So Ms. Mason resumed her dissertation on the subject of cat toys:

"Cat toys are not just fun for cats, they're also educational, especially when the owner is thoughtful enough to provide their cats with a real, living mouse as a toy. This way a cat can have fun while at the same time fulfilling its natural predilection for the Splatter Punk genre."

In all the time he had his cats, Conniff had never been aware that they were fans of Splatter Punk. For the record, Splatter Punk is a form of horror fiction that had a vogue during the 1980s. It was somewhat relevant for the latter part of the 20th century, but then its popularity waned as the country became more politically correct and the citizenry became more attuned to the gentler pleasures of Torture Porn. Conniff, it should be noted, has said for the record that he is not an aficionado of Torture Porn, unless it's well directed and moves the story along.

But if the cat's interest in Splatter Punk was questionable, nobody raised an objection, so Ms. Mason went forward with her point:

"The alleged 'toy' that Mr. Conniff presented his cats with was hardly sufficient. For one thing, it was rubber. Any veterinarian will tell you that real mice are not covered in rubber!"

Just for veracity's sake, we need to clarify that instances of rodents with a rubber fetish are quite rare; if anything, researchers have discovered that mice, while dark and subversive in their everyday activities, tend to be more on the vanilla side when it comes to their sex lives.

But back to Ms. Mason:

"The particular brand of rubber that these toy mice are made of is impossible to fully penetrate with teeth, and that doesn't matter anyway because there is nothing but air inside these pathetic products, no entails or life support system to be instantly severed, thus substantially limiting the fun factor for any cat."

All the spectators in the room nodded their heads and murmured in agreement.

"And then there's that squeak, the annoying noise that the toy makes anytime a cat touches it. What is this supposed to do? Is it meant to be exciting for a cat? Is a cat expected to be all like, 'Oh, boy! I made a fake mouse get all squeaky. What fun! I'm going to write a rave review about it on Yelp!"

"They really seemed to enjoy it," Conniff said, in a lawyerly attempt to rebut her.

"For how long?" Ms. Mason asked.

"Oh, a long time..." Conniff replied.

"Mr. Conniff, I remind you that you are under oath," the judge said.

"Uh, well, um..." Conniff sputtered. "My cats enjoyed the toys I got them." He thought for another moment and then said, almost in a whisper, "for about five minutes."

He quickly sat down, smart enough to know he had made another strategic mistake, but too dumb to realize that he was the lawyer in the case and wasn't technically under oath.

CHAPTER TWENTY

Ms. Mason was not yet finished with her cat toy take-down, but she appeared to be softening her tone:

"Look, I won't deny that Mr. Conniff's apartment does have some fun cat toys, namely the couch, the chairs, the futon and the drapes. Upholstery and textured fabric are like Las Vegas for cats."

She turned to Millie and Barney, perhaps for nods of approval, but they were both preoccupied with the task of avoiding eye contact with the world and not paying attention to anything else except the sheer nothingness they were focused on.

Mason turned back her attention to her opponent. "But Conniff does everything he can to discourage his cats from having their way with the landscape of dreams that are these interior decorations. When the cats climb up the drapes, he says mean, hurtful things, like...wait, I have it here..."

She consulted her notes and then read:

"Hey, get down off those drapes!"

A gasp went up in the courtroom. Ms. Mason waited for the shocked disapproval to die down, then resumed her spiel:

"Had Conniff lived in Paris in the 1920s and had Pablo Picasso been his house pet, there's a good chance many of his Cubist masterpieces might have never seen the light of day. Millie and Barney's work with furniture fabric falls more under the category of Abstract Destructionism, but the suppression of artistic expression is the same in both instances."

"I'm just trying to protect my stuff!" Conniff protested. He then glanced over at the stern looking judge and started to sit back down, but the judge said, "No, go ahead, I can relate, I have stuff."

Ms. Mason's swagger decreased just a notch. She hadn't counted on the possibility that the judge might own stuff, and worse, maybe even enjoyed stuff.

"I can't help it," Conniff said. "I like the things I own. For instance, I have a futon..."

"You know what's sad about that?" Ms. Mason interjected.

"What?"

"It's a futon."

"She's got you there," the judge said. "Futons are inherently sad."

The spectators all nodded knowingly. The stark tragedy of a grown man with a futon was something they were all aware of, and if Conniff had any notion to point out that he was receiving a discourse on sadness from a grown man dressed in a dog costume, he kept it to himself.

"Okay, I admit, futons are nothing fancy," Conniff said. "And they're small, so I sometimes have to stick my feet over the side of the bed when I sleep, and when I do this, Barney always jumps up and viciously bites my ankle. I awaken in a fit of pain, but I somehow manage to put up with this, even though I need my rest so I can have the energy I require to get up and pee several times a night!"

Conniff seemed to immediately realize that there is nothing ever to be gained from telling anyone how many times you pee in the course of an evening. Why he thought this would be a good thing to share was beyond the capacity of basic human understanding.

Mercifully, Ms. Mason changed the subject. "I would like to introduce a tape into evidence," she said.

A big reel to reel tape player was wheeled into the courtroom. It can only be assumed that she was deploying this out-of-date technology for dramatic effect. Having someone hand her an iPhone would not have been as visually striking.

She pressed a button and a sound came out that was truly horrifying.

"This was sent over to us by the national Sleep Apnea Institute," she said. "It is the sound of Mr. Conniff snoring. It is a noise that Millie and Barney have to contend with every night!"

"Objection!" Conniff cried, trying to be heard over the wail of his own snoring. "This is an illegal wiretap! I never authorized the Sleep Apnea Institute or anyone else to come into my house and record me!"

"They did not come to your house," Mason replied. "They recorded you on your futon making these noises in the West Village of Manhattan from all the way across town in their Upper East Side offices!"

Ms. Mason was also barely heard by anyone as she said this, and it wasn't just the assault of Conniff's recorded snoring that dimmed her voice, it was also the cries of despair coming from others in the room. *"Turn it off!!! Turn it off!!!"* one onlooker screamed, sounding like George C. Scott in the movie *Hardcore* as he spots his daughter in an a porno. The cacophony of Conniff's snoring also caused several delicate looking women to curl up into the fetal position, spastically sobbing and feeling a deep need to call their moms. One distraught man spoke for everyone when he pulled at his hair while repeatedly yelling, *"There is no God!"*

The length of the tape was not more than a few moments, but for those assembled in the room, it was as traumatic as binge-watching *Faces of Death* videos. But through it all, two figures in the courtroom registered no reaction at all - Millie and Barney. They continued sleeping, oblivious to everything. For them, Conniff's snoring was like having a roommate who listened to Lou Reed's *Metal Machine Music* every night -- if the room-mate's name is on the lease, there's not much you can do, so you might as well try to get used to it.

Finally Ms. Mason turned the recording off and pointed at the cats. "As you can all see, Millie and Barney are accustomed to this aural atrocity," she said. "But if you had to live with this, wouldn't you bite his ankle?"

Suddenly the entire room shook to the sound of a piercing scream.

"Ahhhhhhhhh!!!"

It was Conniff who made this noise, but it wasn't in response to Ms. Mason, it was in response to the court stenographer, who was on her knees, biting Conniff's ankle as hard as she could.

Ms. Mason fed on the chaos happening in the room, adding intensity to her prosecutorial fury.

"As you can all see, the impulse to assault Conniff's foot while his snoring

attacks your ears is irresistible," she said. "It's proactive, it's cathartic, and a rare example of any living thing taking an interest in Mr. Conniff's body."

If she had had a microphone, she would have dropped it. Conniff, meanwhile, was rubbing his now bloodied ankle. He was handed a first aid kit by the stenographer who had just bit him, not out of any feelings of remorse, but out of a sense of professionalism. It's part of the court stenographer's code: if you bite into a defendant's skin, you help him heal the injury you caused. She also picked the bits of skin she had bitten up off the floor, but that was just because she's a neat freak, it's not a part of the court stenographer's code at all. Either way, as far as Conniff was concerned, he and the stenographer now had a history together, and he wanted to write his phone number on one of the pieces of flesh she was collecting, but he didn't have a pen handy.

In the midst of all this, Millie and Barney were taking a gigantic dump in the box of kitty litter underneath Ms. Mason's table, but not as big as the dump the American justice system appeared to be taking on Mr. Conniff.

There was only so much that one man can take. Conniff had not only been mentally abused, he had now been physically abused as well. The time had come for him to fight back and fight back hard!

But that time passed. Conniff had something in his mind he wanted to say, but then realized that if he wanted a maintain any semblance of being a distinguished lawyer, asking if anyone had any Vicodin was probably not the way to go.

CHAPTER TWENTY-ONE

Now that it had been established that Mr. Conniff does indeed snore, Ms. Mason pivoted to another topic. She knew that if she dwelled on Conniff's sleep patterns, some in the room might come to resent her for exposing them to the horror in the first place.

"I'd like to acknowledge that Millie and Barney are not completely indifferent to the needs of Mr. Conniff," Ms. Mason said. "In fact, on several occasions they have gone above and beyond the usual expectations we have of cats and sometimes actually pretended to give a shit."

This was a bold, not to mention generous, statement for Ms. Mason to make. Cat owners the world over have been known to long for that rare, precious moment when their cats manage to work up the energy to pretend to give a shit about them. It often happens when they hear the click of a can of cat food being flipped open, but most everyone agrees that it is the food that the cats care about, not the person providing the food, although the person providing the food is an unfortunate necessity in the eyes of cats. House cats can either die of starvation or allow humans to feed them, and most cats have come to the conclusion that the latter option is the lesser of two evils.

Food is something that cats actually do care about, but many experts agree that they only pretend to care about human beings, and then only on special occasions, so nobody expected Ms. Mason to suggest in a court of law that Millie and Barney are sometimes prone to pretending to give a shit about Mr. Conniff.

She showed the court some photos.

"Look at this picture of Barney!" she said.

"And check out this picture of Millie!"

"Now look at this picture of Barney and Millie together!"

"Can't you see? Isn't it obvious? They are both pretending to give a shit!"

A collective "*awwww!*" went up among the spectators. The sight of the two cats making an effort to be insincere was truly heartwarming.

But this was just a preamble to Ms. Mason's real point:

"And yet, despite all this, Conniff still saw fit to disparage these cats on Twitter, Facebook and Instagram."

"I'd like to point something out if I may, your honor," Conniff said. Luckily for him, the judge felt a possible infestation of fleas inside his furry ears. He wore these artificial ears with the same sense of dignity that a British Barrister wears a powdered wig, but the illusion of dignity was somewhat diminished whenever he furiously scratched them. So he was momentarily distracted and thus did not stop Conniff from continuing:

"It is generous of Ms. Mason to say that my cats pretend to give a shit about me," Conniff said. "But I will take it a step further."

"You're not going to make any outlandish claims that you can't back up, are you?" Ms. Mason said.

"And I will remind you that you are in a court of law," the Judge added as he began itching his ears with an intensity that caused his left leg to shake.

"I am aware of that, your honor," Conniff said. "But I will say this for the record, and I will say it unequivocally..."

There was a dramatic pause, then Conniff dropped the bombshell:

"My cats tolerate me."

The courtroom exploded with incredulity.

"That's a reckless and dishonest thing to say," Ms. Mason said.

"Prove it!" the Judge ordered.

"Gladly," Conniff said with an arrogant swagger that had previously been missing from his demeanor. He honestly felt that it would be easy for him to show the world that his cats were complicit in a willingness to allow him to exist.

But when he turned towards Millie and Barney, his smug smile immediately went away. The commotion his pronouncement caused was disturbing both cats. They had that scattered RED ALERT! look on their faces that happened during those rare instances when Conniff vacuumed his apartment. Plus their presence in unfamiliar surroundings, and in an usual state of being -- awake -- all contributed to a nervous energy that was not conducive to showing the world that they were capable of getting along with any human, much less the one they despised as a matter of principle.

Conniff went over and tried to pet his cats. Millie swatted her right paw at him and Barney jumped to the floor and scurried under a table.

Another gambit meant to help Conniff's case had backfired.

And speaking of gambits, Ms. Mason had a fresh one up her ointment-covered sleeve.

"How is anybody supposed to believe that these cats would tolerate you, Mr. Conniff," Ms. Mason said. "When you are same man who authorized the removal of their testicles."

It had been a gasp-filled morning in the courtroom, but the gasp that the crowd let out now was the gaspiest gasp yet. Ms. Mason had the balls to drop the "T" word. Like most cat owners, Conniff could not deny that he had allowed a veterinary clinic to go all Dr. Mengele on his pets.

"Everybody does that to their cats!" Conniff pleaded. *"Everybody!"*

"And if everybody jumped off a cliff, would you?" Ms. Mason said.

"At this moment? Yes, absolutely!" Conniff replied, and nobody doubted him.

Whatever else one could say about Conniff's legal maneuvering, you had to respect his honesty.

But nobody did.

CHAPTER TWENTY-TWO

"I would like to enter the cat's medical records as evidence," Ms. Mason said.

"I object!" Conniff declared. "What possible relevance can that have to this case?"

The Judge was rubbing his fake dog ears in careful contemplation. He had just sprinkled flea powder all over his body. This caused an orange dust cloud that provoked a coughing fit from the court stenographer, but she had worked with the judge before and was used to such occurrences. Some had been known to speculate that the judge's problem with fleas was largely psychosomatic. But nobody ever raised this issue with him, because the one time anyone dared to do so, the judge lashed out with a vindictive anger that was only partially because he was suffering from a bad case of worms. Regardless, the lesson was learned: it was not a good idea to confront the judge about his maladies, imagined or otherwise.

"I see your point about the questionable relevance of the cat's medical records," the judge said to Conniff, who then turned to Mason to express a look of triumph, but before he could form even the beginnings of a sneer on his face, the judge added, "but I'm going to allow Ms. Mason to enter it as evidence."

"Why?!!!" Conniff asked, like a condemned man wondering how come the pudding he requested was left off his last meal.

"I don't know," the judge replied. "What can I tell you, I'm in a quirky, offbeat mood today. Don't you ever just feel like doing stuff with no rhyme or reason sometimes?"

This attitude seemed at odds with the spirit of a court of law, but a committee at an internal hearing later determined that it would be a shame to stifle the judge's free spirited sense of jocularity. This hearing had come about as a result of another trial, where some observers thought the judge's eccentric antics had distracted him from his sacred duty as an arbiter of justice. But the committee ruled in the Judge's favor, even though DNA evidence later exonerated the young man he had sent to the gas chamber.

But the judge could laugh about it now, and Ms. Mason was laughing along with him, and the fact that she was even laughing in the first place forged a bond with the judge that she hoped would last beyond the trial. "I love your irreverent take on the world, Your Honor," she said. "And I encourage you to trust your instincts and goof it up."

"Thank you!" the judge said. "Remind me to hug you later."

They both smiled at each other and Conniff sat down and rubbed his aching ankle. He couldn't tell if the ache was from his gout or from the bite the stenographer had given him. Either way, he was grateful that the physical pain was giving him something to think about besides how much he was being screwed over.

Ms. Mason held up medical records for all to see. "I would like everyone in this room to take note that these cats were both sent against their wills by Mr. Conniff to the veterinarian's office for a day spay. They were subjected to what only can be described as a bizzaro-world bar mitzvah, because the end result of this depraved rite of passage was the opposite of 'Today I am a man!'"

"I'm not Jewish, and neither are my cats," Conniff said, quickly adding, "not that there's anything wrong with being Jewish, but I was raised Catholic so I keep a non-kosher house."

"And you feel qualified to speak on behalf of your cats' religious beliefs?" Ms. Mason asked.

"As far as I know, they're atheists."

A din of skepticism rose up from the spectators, but not the kind of skepticism that atheists engage in. To those assembled in the room, it seemed hard to believe that Millie and Barney were atheists, especially since no one had ever heard them incessantly go on and on and on and on and on and on about being atheists.

"Why do you say that Millie and Barney are atheists?" Ms. Mason asked.

"Hey, they don't even recognize the validity of my existence, so I doubt if they think God exists," Conniff said.

"Good point," the Judge said, and Ms. Mason knew better than to pursue this line of thought any further. It was good sportsmanship to let Conniff have this one.

But now she was ready to get to her main point, and once she did, Conniff came to believe that there was in fact no such thing as a kind and caring God, although he tried to suppress this thought, because if a kind and caring God did exist after all, he didn't want him knowing that he didn't think he existed anymore. Such was the tortured and complex nature of his thinking, which is another way of saying he was losing his freaking mind.

CHAPTER TWENTY-THREE

"I would like to return to the brutal fact that Mr. Conniff had these cats' testicles removed shortly after they were born," Ms. Mason said.

"I was being responsible!" Conniff protested. "It's compassionate, one of the most Sarah McLaughlin things you can possibly do!"

"Be that as it may," she continued, "I'd like you all to please take a moment to imagine a scenario."

"Oh, jeez," Conniff could be heard muttering under his breath. His day was stressful enough, the last thing he was in the mood for was a scenario.

"Just imagine that you are roommates with a nice and friendly enough fellow," Ms. Mason said. "And everything about this person is perfectly acceptable. Except for one thing. Sometime in your your early years, he arranged to have your testicles removed. And let's say he did this because he thought it was the right thing to do. He was even told by the best minds of his generation that he was being responsible by doing this. In fact, there was no way you could fault him on reasonable grounds. But still, knowing all this, wouldn't your first thought always be, no matter what - 'You bastard! How could you do this to me? You're a Junk Removal Service that I never asked for!"

Everyone in the courtroom nodded their heads in agreement, even the several people in the room who had themselves authorized the spaying and neutering of their cats. But none of that mattered because Ms. Mason was mesmerizing; it was as if Michelle Obama was giving an inspiring speech about animal scrotums.

"This is not the type of thing any normal living being would ever get over," Ms. Mason said. 'Sure, you took away my balls, but at least you provide me with water and flavorless dry food' is not a thought has has even once provided anyone with comfort. And if you clogged up your toilet and a plumber came over and cleaned up all your poop, you would probably withhold your gratitude if he also removed your sexual organs while he was at it!"

She was making her case with surgical precision, which was somewhat ironic, considering the subject matter. What any of this had to do with defamation of character, which is what this trial was originally supposed to be about, was anybody's guess, but she seemed on the verge of sewing up a victory for herself and for Millie and Barney.

But then she made a misstep, and it was the first time things went in Mr. Conniff's favor since the trial began. If Conniff played his cards right, he could finally turn things around, as long as he didn't blow it.

Needless to say, he totally blew it.

CHAPTER TWENTY-FOUR

Conniff had lost all hope that he would be able to make an effective case on his own behalf, but out of sheer desperation he stood up and said, "What about dogs?"

The room became silent, and everyone looked up at the judge, whose dog costume was now more conspicuous than ever.

"What about dogs?" the Judge said in a voice devoid of all emotion, like a stoic assassin agreeing to carry out a contract on someone's life.

But at this point Conniff felt he had nothing to lose, so he dove head-first into a shallow puddle of puppy piss. "Dogs have had their junk removed just as often as cats," he said.

("Junk," it should be noted, is the euphemism people use to describe the part of the anatomy known as the ding-a-ling.)

Conniff continued:

"Yet dogs don't walk through life with a chip on their shoulder. They don't sit around the house and mope all day. They find reasons to be enthusiastic. They experience the joy in jumping up and down, greeting people at the door, barking at the mailman, wagging their tails, eating cat turds, you name it. They don't..."

Conniff stopped and thought for a moment.

"Wow, it suddenly occurs to me - how come I don't have a dog?"

The judge laughed appreciatively, and this made it okay for everyone else in the courtroom to laugh as well.

"You make great point," the judge said, still laughing. Everyone else continued to laugh.

It was the first time since the trial started that Conniff had received any kind of positive reinforcement from the judge, and Ms. Mason was not about to let this moment go unchallenged, which is probably why she spoke without taking a second to think about what she was saying:

"Dogs don't complain about being neutered because dogs are dumb," she said.

The laughter in the room abruptly ended.

"Oh, Your Honor, I didn't mean to..." she started to say.

Her voice was drowned out by the whimpering of the judge, and that was drowned out by the harsh pounding of his gavel.

"Court is in recess for fifteen minutes," he said. "I need to go to the park and relieve myself"

There had been complaints from community groups that the judge's habit of going across the street to the public park to go to the bathroom on the lawn was adversely affecting the quality of life in the neighborhood, despite his reassurances that he always cleaned up after himself and that sanitizing his ass by wiping it along the grass made for good mulch, but at this moment none of that mattered.

What did matter, at least to Mr. Conniff, was that he finally had an opening to fight back and maybe, just maybe win his case.

It seemed as if the fates were finally smiling down on Mr. Conniff.

But as you will soon find out, the fates were just dicking him around.

CHAPTER TWENTY-FIVE

During the recess, the general feeling in the courtroom was that Ms. Mason had made a grievous misstep, and no one believed this more than Ms. Mason. She paced frantically back and forth, all the while apologizing profusely to Millie and Barney. Whatever their thoughts were about this, they were keeping them close to the vest. Millie was staring at something and Barney was staring at something else, and not a single person in that room could have told you what the hell they were staring at. If Ms. Mason was annoyed that Barney and Millie had chosen this moment to stare into the abyss, she wasn't expressing any displeasure with them; all of her re-criminations at that moment were directed towards herself. Plus, she knew that staring into the abyss was a favorite activity for cats, and that the many hours they spend face to face with a gaping nothingness that represents the futility of existence is part of what makes them so darn adorable.

But much more so than the cats, it was the judge that she really wanted to apologize to; however, he was still in the park across the street; in fact he could be viewed through the courtroom window on the lawn as he was excavating his bodily waste while having an affable conservation with a first year law student who happened to walk by. The young man, hairless save for the pointy crew cut on his head, and wearing a Men's Warehouse business suit with reckless abandon, was a stark contrast to the be-co-splayed judge. They were discussing the ethical issues raised by a man taking advantage of public health ordinances that do not apply to animals. It's something Louis Brandies never had to grapple with, mainly because as far as anybody knew, he had long felt it was proper jurisprudence to always use indoor facilities when he pinched out a loaf.

But the question of what rights of public defecation does a man wearing a dog costume have was a hot button issue, or, perhaps more appropriately, a hot box issue, to this particular judge.

"If I came out here in my regular business suit and pulled down my pants and took a crap in the middle of the park, I could be cited for public indecency," the earnest young law student said to the judge. "But you say the fact that you're wearing a dog outfit makes it okay? Don't you see the legal grey area?"

"It's more of a brown area," the judge replied as he scooped up his own mess with his plastic glove-covered hand. "But you do raise a valid concern. It is something I wrestle with every day. I've often pontificated on the moral conundrum - is it okay for a man with hemorrhoids to scream 'my ass is on fire' in a crowded theater? I've never come up with a satisfying answer, but I am thankful that bright young men like you are asking these questions."

He shook the young man's hand and the young man seemed grateful for the older, wiser judge's approval, even though the hand he just shook was covered in excrement -- human excrement -- which brought him back to the central thesis he had raised in the first place. Still, he felt that it had been an intellectually satisfying conversation, even though the judge had literally shit all over his argument.

But the judge was now on his way back to the courtroom, and what he planned to say had the potential to not just impact this trial, but every subsequent trial for the remainder of the twenty-first century.

But when he got to the bench he forgot what he was going to say, so instead the trial just continued on as before.

CHAPTER TWENTY-SIX

Seconds after the judge banged the gavel, bringing the court back into session (and startling the cats to the point where they looked away from whatever it was they were looking at for a moment before they resumed looking at whatever it was again), Ms. Mason began her plea for forgiveness.

"Your Honor, I'm so sorry for what I said," she began. "I didn't mean to say that dogs are dumb. I...uh, I just wonder why they don't have contempt for the human race the way cats do."

This seemed an odd thing to say, and it was clear from the satisfied grimace on Conniff's face that he was thinking, "yeah, that's it, just keep digging a deeper hole."

And keep digging she did. "Cats, unlike dogs, seem to understand that the human race is a species that is destroying the planet, so isn't the attitude that cats have towards humans the proper attitude? Once the planet has been weened of its natural resources, there will be no more reproducing, so in many ways what humans have been doing for years to cats and dogs is what humans are are now doing to Earth as a whole."

Much to everyone's surprise, a smile formed on the judge's face, causing his painted on whiskers to point upwards, as if they were forming quotation marks around his nose. "You make a good point, young lady," he said. "I forgive you for saying what you said. Because, after all, who is more forgiving than a dog?"

A collective *"awwww"* came up from the crowd, but Conniff was having none of it.

"But you're not a dog!" he shouted, once again picking exactly the right moment to say exactly the wrong thing. "Your Honor, I mean no disrespect," he continued in a tone that came off as quite disrespectful. "I would just like to make some of the points I wanted to make when you were still mad at my opponent. I wanted to have an opportunity to get on your good side while Ms. Mason was still on your bad side."

Conniff's inexperience as a lawyer was never more apparent than at this moment, but still, the judge was in a generous mood. "Go ahead," he said. "Give it your best shot."

"Okay, here goes," Conniff said. "Look, even though I am the proud roommate of two cats, people seem to be questioning whether I'm a real cat person."

"Uh, yeah, no kidding?" Mason said in a singsongy valley girl tone of voice that was uncharacteristic of her, but had its desired impact at this moment.

"I am a cat person!" Conniff said. "But if I fell down a well, it would be a dog that I'd hope might wander by so I could ask it to go get help. As much as I love Millie and Barney, they would be useless in a situation like this. I mean, come on, has a cat ever saved a person's life? And when a crazy cat lady with fifty cats dies, it never occurs to even one of them to pick up a phone and tell the coroner to come over. And you've heard of cases where an eccentric wealthy cat owner dies and leaves all of his or her wealth to a cat, right? Well, in most cases, the cat who inherited all that wealth blows it all in a matter of months. It's a known fact that dogs make much shrewder investments with their money. They're smart that way."

Conniff looked around the courtroom, but if he was expecting nods of approval, all he got were perplexed stares from the spectators, not to mention Millie and Barney, who were gazing at him like he was an idiot. Conniff was not taken aback by this because this was the way his cats always looked at him.

Conniff then made an unwise choice. He resumed speaking:

"It is true that unlike cats, dogs have to be taken outside to go to the bathroom, but this is just another example of their intelligence. They've figured out a way to trick their owners into letting them see the world, or at least the radius around their house. Plus they get to meet people and make contacts with other dogs who could possibly help their careers. Cats look at their poop as just that: poop. Dogs look at their poop as business cards. When a dog takes a crap in the street, he's not just taking a crap in the street, he's networking."

Not a single person in the room had any idea what Mr. Conniff's point was, including, and perhaps especially, Mr. Conniff.

"Look, Your Honor," he said in conclusion. "I just wanted to show the court that I'm capable of saying things with a cadence in my voice that makes me sound all lawyerly and stuff."

The judge was looking at his phone, and it was a few moments before he finally glanced up at Mr. Conniff.

"Were you talking?" he distractedly said. Then, before Conniff could answer, he added, "Oh, yeah, right," as if suddenly remembering a thankless chore he was supposed to do. "Look, I only let you speak because I needed to check my email. Needless to say, please have whatever the hell Conniff just said stricken from the record."

The spectators breathed a collective sigh of relief and the trial resumed.

But Conniff, unbeknownst to anyone else, still had an ace up his sleeve.

It was left over from a card trick he had performed at an audition, and it didn't do him a damn bit of good now.

CHAPTER TWENTY-SEVEN

The next statement Ms. Mason made was unexpected coming as it did from an opponent of Mr. Conniff.

"I would like to point out that Mr. Conniff was once an alcoholic and a drug addict and he has admirably maintained his sobriety for over thirty years."

Everyone in the room clapped loudly, including the judge. Such moments went to the core of why Conniff had stayed devoted to sobriety for so many years: it was always good for an applause break.

Conniff accepted the cheers gracefully. His eyes scanned the room for interested looks on the faces of women so he could, as he often did during his many years of recovery, attempt to use the spiritual strength he gained from his 12 step program as a means of getting laid.

Once the applause died down, Ms. Mason continued. "I bring this up only to point out that his sobriety, as worthy of respect as it is, has made him a lousy cat owner."

"*What?!!!*" Conniff said, banging his fist on the table in the petulant way of a man who desperately needs a drink.

"I've done some research into Mr. Conniff's past history, and have found out a few facts that I think are relevant," she said.

"*Objection!*" Conniff said. "My criminal record is immaterial!"

"Criminal record?" Ms. Mason said. "Who said anything about a criminal record? I didn't know you had one."

"A criminal record? Hmm, interesting." the judge said, staring at Conniff with the kind of severe glare that usually precedes the words, "you're grounded, young man."

"I...uh...it was no big deal," Conniff said. "Possession of pot. Back in the seventies. It was stricken from the record. It scared me straight. I haven't taken a drug since."

"Then why did you bring it up?" the judge demanded.

"I... I'm high!"

It was immediately obvious to everyone that this was a lie said in a moment of panic, but an investigation later done by this reporter revealed that Conniff's drug bust in the seventies was indeed erased from his record. It was something he had done that was not known to the general public, so in that sense it was good preparation for his show business career.

Conniff had in fact been arrested for possession of pot. It was a small amount, and the judge in the case was going to let him off with a warning, but then cited him, not for taking the drug, but for actually enjoying the album *Tales From Topographic Oceans* by the prog-rock band Yes while under the influence of the drug. At the time, Conniff was given the option of cutting a deal where he could publicly renounce his love of that two-record set and instead endorse *Dark Side of the Moon* by Pink Floyd as the greatest prog album ever. Much to everyone's shock, Conniff refused to capitulate and to this day insists that Yes are the far greater band, which might help explain why he lives alone with two cats.

Conniff's court-appointed lawyer at the time refused to continue representing him when he was made aware of this fact, but Conniff was later able to successfully have the lawyer's license revoked when he proved conclusively that when he was high, he liked to listen to thematic prog-rock concept albums like *The Six Wives of Henry the 8th* by Rick Wakeman.

Ultimately, neither Conniff nor his lawyer were penalized any further, because the court decreed that listening to those albums was considered community service.

The whole thing was a mess that was swept under the rug. Conniff has never spoken of it since, although he has continued to listen to and love prog-rock even without drugs, but this is a matter for a psychiatrist, not a lawyer.

Bringing up the transgressions of his past was only the latest in a series of missteps Conniff had made during the trial. At this moment, Conniff seemed almost defeated. But there was one factor that people hadn't counted on. People like Conniff, with thirty-plus years of sobriety, are strong individuals with tremendous reserves of inner-strength People like Conniff are not likely to so easily fold under adversity.

But we are not talking about Conniff, we're talking about people *like* Conniff. Conniff himself was overwhelmed by all the adversity and was ready to fold like laundry.

CHAPTER TWENTY-EIGHT

Ms. Mason made her next statement in a calm, measured voice, never tipping her hand that what she was about to reveal would be a ninja death kick.

"Did you all know that when Mr. Conniff was a child, he lived with a mother who hated cats?"

The Judge banged his gavel to silence the outrage that went up among the spectators. He would have sent someone out to buy smelling salts if he had any idea where the hell a person would go to buy smelling salts. (Ye Old Movie Prop Shop on route 340, Lancaster, PA, according to research done by the author.)

"What is this?" Conniff protested. "I thought you were going to be talking about my drug use."

"Oh, we'll get to your Emerson, Lake and Palmer fandom in a moment."

(Ms. Mason knew nothing about Conniff's love of *Tales From Topographic Oceans*, that testimony was part a sealed document, she only knew in vague, general terms that he loved prog, so she made an educated guess about Emerson, Lake and Palmer, which of course proved to be correct.)

"What I want to focus on right now is that you grew up in an environment hostile to cats, and it is my contention that you brought that hostility into your adult life, as your mean-spirited tweets about Millie and Barney clearly show," Ms. Mason said.

"I admit my mom didn't like cats," Conniff said. "She had been brought up during the Depression, so when cats shed, it reminded her of the Dust Bowl."

"Your mother grew up in a Southampton mansion," Mason retorted. "How would she know about the Dust Bowl?"

"Well," Conniff said. "Uh..." he didn't have an answer ready so he spent an awkward moment wracking his brain for one. "Um... late in life, she saw *The Grapes of Wrath* on a big screen, high definition TV, and it really brought the hardships of Okie farmers to life, so she knew plenty about the Dust Bowl."

There was a silence in the court. Everyone was stunned by the stupidity of what had just been said.

"There were no high-def TVs when you were growing up," Ms. Mason said. "So that has no relevance to the fact that you were raised in a household that was hostile to cats."

"My mom was hostile to cats, I wasn't, " Conniff said. "I always wanted a cat."

"Oh, so you're saying your childhood dog wasn't good enough?"

"Silky? My beloved childhood dog?" Conniff said, his voice choking up. "Silky was the greatest pet ever. Do you know how traumatic my childhood was? My dad was sick with a stroke, he was paralyzed and couldn't move. My mom suffered from mental illness and was in and out of hospitals, she had shock treatments, was over-prescribed medication, you name it, the worst. And I couldn't cope and had no guidance so naturally I turned to drugs and threw my youth away. But through it all, Silky was always there, always ready to lick my face and make me smile and feel warm and safe with uninhibited, unconditional love. So don't tell me that Silky wasn't good enough. She was the best of all time."

"Better than Millie and Barney?"

"Are you kidding me? Of course Silky was a better pet than Millie and Barney. I..."

Conniff stopped himself right there. He had fallen into Ms. Mason's trap. Everyone was glaring at him as if this was Nuremberg and he was testifying that he was only following orders.

"But, honestly, I love my cats. I..."

He looked over at his cats. If their feelings were hurt by his statement that he didn't love them as much as he loved his childhood dog, they weren't showing it. Luckily for Conniff, he said this at a moment when they were distracted because they were lost in their own heads not giving a shit about a completely unrelated topic.

But if Conniff had escaped judgment from his cats, the people in this courtroom were a different matter entirely. He could feel their harsh disapproval burning into him like a tattoo of the word asshole. He was ready to give up. He sat back down.

Ms. Mason felt sorry for him. "I'm going to refrain from bringing up your love of Emerson, Lake and Palmer any further," she said.

"I'm actually more into Yes and King Crimson, but... oh, never mind."

Now, more than ever, Conniff needed a miracle. And maybe, just maybe, a miracle was waiting for him, just around the corner.

But it wasn't. Not at all.

CHAPTER TWENTY-NINE

Conniff was being rhetorically slapped around by Ms Mason's legal expertise, and she hadn't even yet gotten to the original point she wanted to make about his drug use.

"As an adolescent, Mr. Conniff spent a lot of time smoking bong hits and giggling at his dog's delightful antics," she said. "And what is it that delighted him so? The sight of his dog licking his crotch."

The stoned people in the room -- which an informal survey revealed to be just about everyone -- all giggled at this. Just the thought of a dog licking its crotch is pretty funny if you're sober and Oscar Wilde-level wit if you're baked.

Except, apparently, in the case of Mr. Conniff.

"And this brings us to one of the biggest complaints against Conniff by the cats." Ms. Mason said. "They lick their crotches all the time and Mr. Conniff has not so much as giggled even once."

Everyone stared at Conniff's lifeless, sober face and knew exactly what she was talking about.

"Mr. Conniff no longer smokes pot, so watching his pets lick themselves in the places where their private parts used to be is no longer amusing to him. Without the artificial stimulants that he has so admirably avoided for most of his adult life, he has lost the ability to see the entertainment value in things that aren't entertaining. As a sober, recovering person with a responsible approach to life, he finds more satisfaction in structured forms, like pornography."

"Why bring porn into it?" Conniff asked. "My hobbies are my own business."

"Oh, are they?" Mason responded in a voice heavy with accusation. "I will now prove that porn is more than just a hobby to you, that you tried to make money by creating *CAT PORN SITES!*"

The room erupted in umbrage. Conniff turned to the crowd and tried to quell their gasps of disbelief.

"You've got it all wrong!" he said. "It's called the entrepreneurial spirit! And these sites were not for the entertainment of people! They were for the entertainment of cats!"

This did not calm anyone down in the least bit. But further investigation revealed that what he was saying was true: the websites he created were meant for cats. And although the idea of creating erotic content for creatures without testicles is a bit on the absurd side, equally so for outdoor cats who may still have their sexual organs intact, but are never on the Internet due to the unreliability of wi-fi in the wilderness, it didn't stop Mr. Conniff from doing exactly what Ms. Mason was accusing him of.

Ms. Mason had a big TV screen wheeled in and displayed excerpts from the websites Conniff had created meant for the adult arousal of house cats, along with descriptions written on the sites:

GROOM BABY GROOM
Extreme self-cleaning with cats who can't stop licking themselves all over. This is some of the dirtiest cleaning you are ever going to see.

CAT CUCKS
Cats who get off on seeing other cats eat food that was meant for them.

PECKROPHELIA
House Cats who don't know the joy of capturing birds, bringing them home, presenting them to a human, and then having their way with them will live vicariously through these slow-paced cat-on-bird power-play scenarios.

CATS DOIN' IT DOGGIE STYLE

Not necessarily what you think. Cats who get off on acting like dogs, treating their human owners as if they care about them. Most cats consider this to be the sickest and most depraved porn site there is.

BELLY RUB HUB

Nothing but cats getting belly rubs, 24/7. Considered soft core, but on the other hand, when you don't have any sexual equipment, this is as hard core as it gets.

DON'T TOUCH ME THERE!

Videos of cats being touched in that one place that makes them go nuts and suddenly attack their owner. Money shot is humans screaming in agony as they are scratched.

KITTIES BEHIND BARS

Cats sitting in cat cages while Sarah McLaughlin songs play. *Warning: This is some sick shit.*

VOYEURS VITTLES

Shots of cats watching blankly and with complete disinterest as humans have sex offscreen.

OPEN WIDE, BABY!

Just a locked-down shot of can opener opening a can of cat food. Against every law of nature, neutered cats have been known to ejaculate while watching this.

Ms. Mason displayed the clips from these sites to the assembled onlookers, but if she was expecting more outrage, she was disappointed. Most of the spectators found the clips quite entertaining and a couple of stoned-out dudes in the back indulged in self-pleasuring, although to their credit, they did so quietly.

"I'd watch that," the judge was heard to mutter after one of the clips.

"I admit I marketed these sites to the wrong demographic," Conniff said. "I thought that cats would enjoy them, but cats don't get off on watching cats, humans get off on watching cats."

Conniff spoke a universal truth, but Ms. Mason was not about to let him have any sort of persuasion with the judge "Like your tweets and Facebook status updates, this all still goes under the heading of cat exploitation," she said.

"But is it illegal?" Conniff asked.

The judge banged his gavel. "What the hell does that have to do with anything?" he asked. "Questions of legality and illegality have no place in a court of law."

Ms. Mason saw this as her opening to bring her prosecution of Conniff up to the next level.

"Your Honor, I now would like to present to you the only testimony that matters. The testimony of Millie and Barney."

Even a casual observer had to believe that what was about to take place would be the part of the trial that would go down in history.

But that guy left the trial before the testimony happened, because, as was reported, he was only a casual observer.

CHAPTER THIRTY

"I now call to the stand, Barney," Ms. Mason said with as much gravitas as was possible for a woman asking a cat to testify in a court of law.

It surprised no one who was following this trial that Barney had been sleeping when he was called to the stand. He had been sleeping for about 99% of the time since the trial began. Waking Barney up caused him great annoyance, and when he glared at Ms. Mason, who was clumsily shaking him, it looked like he might be willing to switch sides. For all his consternation towards Conniff, he at least knew that in his apartment, Conniff was not prone to waking him on purpose, since he was also asleep a great deal of the time as well.

Barney's disgruntlement as Ms. Mason carried him to the stand was clear for all to see. He was placated somewhat when he was given some Psychic Diet cat food to eat. Once he had eaten a decent portion of the bowl, Barney began his testimony, meaning he began throwing up large amounts of alphabet puke.

Ms. Mason posed her first question:

"Barney, tell us up a little something about your background."

Barney vomited the following on the floor:

I WAS BORN INTO A LARGE LITTER OF OFFSPRING TO A MOTHER WHO DID NOT LET THE NORMS OF SOCIETY RULE HER THINKING. SEXUAL PROMISCUITY AMONG FELINES IS FROWNED UPON BY THE MAN. BUT MY MOM WAS ALL ABOUT EMPOWERMENT.

"Excuse me, but that doesn't sound like the type of thing Barney would say," Conniff said. "I think he was coached by his lawyer."

"His words have been regurgitated onto the floor, plain for everyone to see," Mason said.

"Well, I demand that Barney's words be stricken from the record, or at least covered in sawdust or cleaned up with a paper towel," Conniff said.

"It's not your place to demand anything!" the Judge said. "The puke is sustained!"

Ms. Mason continued questioning Barney:

"So your mother was able to give birth to you, at least partly because she still had her sexual organs. That is wonderful. What was your life with her like?"

Barney then vomited these words:

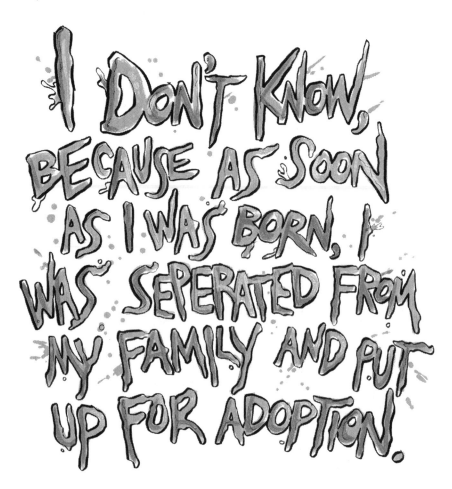

I DON'T KNOW, BECAUSE AS SOON AS I WAS BORN, I WAS SEPERATED FROM MY FAMILY AND PUT UP FOR ADOPTION.

"In other words..."

Another spew of chunks, then:

Everyone gasped.

"No more questions," Ms Mason said.

Ending his testimony was a strategic move on her part. She felt that Barney had said enough, and his puke was stinking up the place something awful, so more vomit might turn the court against him. Entering cat vomit into testimony was a new, uncharted area in the American Judicial System, so Ms. Mason was treading carefully, a wise move according to most legal analysts.

Conniff stepped up for his cross-examination, but Barney was now sound asleep, curled up in a ball with his paw covering his head.

It is so adorable when Barney, or any other cat for that matter, does the whole sleeping with paws over the eyes thing. Only with great reluctance is a cat's sleep disturbed under this circumstance. But Conniff was in no position to play it safe. He had to boldly step forward and aggressively interrogate his cat. Otherwise, he could lose everything. This was one of those moments in life that demand real courage.

"No questions," Conniff said, and then he quietly sat back down in his seat.

CHAPTER THIRTY-ONE

Perhaps realizing that his overall wussiness was hurting his chances, Conniff stood up and asked everyone to recognize that most cats have an overall sense of the basic tragic nature of life, so he should not be blamed for his cat's sour disposition.

"Need I remind everyone that in the story *Metamorphosis*, the main character turns into a cockroach," he said. "Because if the character had turned into a cat, the dimensions of the story would have been too dark for even Kafka to deal with."

If Conniff thought he was making a good point, it was immediately pounced on by Ms. Mason.

"What you are saying is not Kafkaesque, it's Kalfkadiculous!" she said. "I for one would have loved reading a story called *MeowMorphosis*. I think it would have been adorable! And it just so happens that Kafka's recent biographers have revealed that he loved cat calendars and had a huge collection of Hello Kitty merchandise," she said. "And it was a mutual admiration society: the founder of Hello Kitty owned the world's largest stockpile of Hello Kafka memorabilia."

To Conniff, this all sounded a bit on the historically inaccurate side. But Ms. Mason was such a mesmerizing speaker that contradicting her seemed like a daunting task; plus, the faces of everyone in the room had become imbued with a warm glow, like they were all having Christmas dinner with a family of velvet clowns. The darkness implied by Conniff was an unwelcome intrusion in their soft world of cuddly cat preciousness.

"I think right now would be a good time to call Millie to the stand," Ms.

Mason said.

Conniff was fully aware of the potentially damning nature of Millie's testimony. A bold gambit to outmaneuver his opponent was what was called for. Nothing less would do.

But he couldn't think of anything, so he sat back down and pretended to look over his notes on a blank legal pad.

CHAPTER THIRTY-TWO

Ms. Mason went to grab Millie off the top of the table, but Millie saw her approach, hissed like a steam engine, then jumped down to the floor. There was a brief moment when it seemed that getting Millie to testify would be a problem, but by her own volition she scurried forward and jumped up onto the witness stand.

It was cute as hell so of course everyone happily sighed, except for Conniff, who in the past had delighted at the sight of Millie's frenzied scurrying, but in this setting saw it as more of an adorable Bataan Death March.

"Okay, Millie," Ms. Mason said. "Tell us your story."

She ate her Psychic Diet cat food and puked the following:

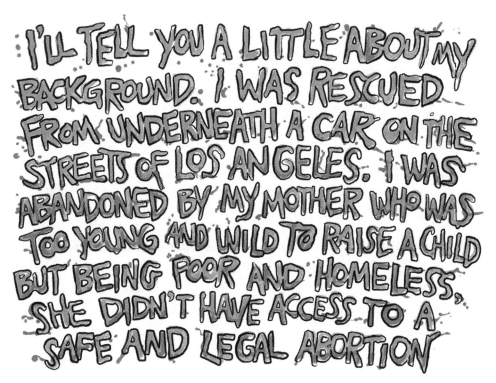

I'LL TELL YOU A LITTLE ABOUT MY BACKGROUND. I WAS RESCUED FROM UNDERNEATH A CAR ON THE STREETS OF LOS ANGELES. I WAS ABANDONED BY MY MOTHER WHO WAS TOO YOUNG AND WILD TO RAISE A CHILD BUT BEING POOR AND HOMELESS, SHE DIDN'T HAVE ACCESS TO A SAFE AND LEGAL ABORTION

This made everyone in the room a bit uncomfortable, but Conniff saw it as a chance to score some points.

"Well, I for one am glad you weren't aborted, Millie," he said.

"Would you please leave your alt-right political agenda out of this?" Ms. Mason snapped.

"But, I wasn't..." Conniff started to say.

"Ms. Mason, please let Millie continue with her testimony," the judge said. "Conniff's racism is immaterial at this moment."

"I'm not right wing and I'm not racist!" Conniff protested. "Have you seen my twitter feed?"

"Yes, that's the whole reason we're here," Ms. Mason said.

"But most of my tweets express a liberal point of view," he said.

"Who cares," the judge said. "I have a twitter feed, but all we've heard about are your tweets. Do you even follow me on Twitter?"

"Uh..." Conniff began. It was immediately clear that Conniff did not follow the judge on Twitter and there was no point lying about it.

"I'm sorry Your Honor," he said. "As soon as I log on again, I will be sure to..."

"I go to your timeline every day, your honor," Ms. Mason said. "I loved the picture you posted of your lunch. Those steakums looked delicious. And such an elegant dog food bowl."

"I designed it myself," the judge said, smiling at the memory. "It's such an elegant treat to eat that way without being bogged down by distracting annoyances like silverware."

Ms. Mason smiled even more broadly than the judge, then she turned to Millie and said, "When Mr. Conniff started writing nasty tweets about you and Barney, you decided you could tolerate him no longer, is that correct?"

Millie took a big bite of the Psychic Diet cat food, then another. It was expected that her next puking would be as articulate as it was odiferous.

And Millie did indeed vomit up a big pile of puke. But that's all it was - puke. It did not form into words, and thus did not offer any testimony. Whatever Mille had to say was locked inside her head -- her thoughts were now just as mysterious as the inner-workings of every cat's brain, which we know contain some of the most inscrutable thoughts of all God's creatures.

106

"Excuse me, Your Honor, there's something wrong," Ms Mason said. She picked up the box of cat food and examined it.

"Oh, I see what the problem is," she said. "This food is past its expiration date. I'll take some of the food in Barney's bowl and see if that works."

She went over to the table where Barney was. He sat sphinx-like with his two paws on the rim of his food bowl. Ms. Mason went to grab his food and Barney hissed and scratched her hand with a swiftness that one wouldn't expect from such a fat lump of cat.

"Ow! Barney, you poopie head!" Ms. Mason screamed.

It was a thoughtless thing to say, and understandable in the heat of the moment, but still, hearing such language coming out of Ms. Mason's mouth was a bit of a shock for everyone in the courtroom.

Once the gasps of the onlookers died down, Ms. Mason turned to the judge and said, "I'm sorry, Your Honor. I shouldn't have lowered the level of discourse like that. I'll bring Millie over to the food dish and let her eat it from there."

"I wouldn't do that if I were you," Conniff said, but Ms. Mason ignored him.

Meanwhile, the judge said, "Will the bailiff please clean up Millie's cat puke? Ms. Mason's blood is dripping all over it, so now it's disgusting."

In normal circumstances, an officer of the court would resent having to clean up such a mess, but this particular bailiff saw it as an opportunity for stage time.

"Housework is such a drag, am I right, ladies?" he said to the assembled throng as he grabbed a roll of paper towels.

But the judge was in no mood. He shined the light from his iPhone at the bailiff and gave him a signal to wrap it up.

"That's my time, I'm outta here!" the bailiff said, and then he wiped the paper towels on the mess Millie had made and scooped it up with a flour-ish. It was supposed to be his big closer, but working with props wasn't really his forte so he barely even got a smattering of applause.

And people were more focused on Ms. Mason anyway. She tried to pick up Millie, and for her troubles, she received a scratch on her other hand that was twice as savage as the previous scratch from Barney.

"Bitch!" she screamed. Then, she immediately tried to soften her vulgarity with politeness. "I'm sorry," she announced. "I should have said, 'bitch, please.'"

Millie jumped down from the witness stand, then ran over and leaped up onto the table and stood next to Barney.

"I think Millie and Barney should be put in their cat carriers for the remainder of the trial," the judge said. He motioned for the bailiff to go over and grab the cats. The bailiff was happy to be the center of attention again -- he had a couple new bits he wanted to try -- but as he approached the table, Millie and Barney both raised their paws and swiped them in the air, indicating for all to see that they were not going back into confinement without a fight.

Later, many wondered why the cats had willingly gotten into cat carriers to come to the trial, but were now reluctant to do so again. This wasn't hard to figure out. They had initially been excited about the trial but once they were there, they had grown bored and didn't want to be bothered while they thought about other things that were nobody else's business but their own. They had reached that point where they were ready to indulge in that most basic of cat rituals - the unprovoked hissy fit.

Millie and Barney stood side by side on the table, ready to take on all comers. In another setting, this might have been endearing, like an all-cat version of *Kill Bill*, but here, at this particular moment, the threat of actual physical violence greatly diminished the "aw, cute!" factor.

Ms. Mason was still bleeding and in a considerable amount of pain, not just from the cats scratching her, but also from the burden of her allergic reaction to the cats, which had taken a toll. Her eyes were bloodshot, her nose was clogged almost to the point of suffocation, and her skin had been distorted to the point where everyone who looked at her suspected they might be tripping on LSD, and once they realized they weren't high on acid, they sought out the drug anyway to alter their consciousness because the reality of what they were looking at was none too pleasant. Ms. Mason had bravely fought against her allergic affliction, and her oratory had not yet been affected by it. But now, for the first time since the trial started, she seemed at a loss for words.

In comparison, Conniff appeared to have it all together, which meant the world had indeed become ass-backwards. He walked over to the table and nonchalantly began petting Millie and Barney along their backs in regular rhythmic motions. Both cats immediately became less defensive and sat down. Their faces registered no pleasure, or any other emotion except a relative calmness that hadn't been apparent just moments earlier. There was no denying that Conniff was petting them and they were actively allowing him to do so.

"Do you see?" Conniff announced to everyone in the room. "Let the record show this undeniable truth about my cats: They tolerate me! They really, really tolerate me!"

No one questioned the validity of what he was saying. Millie and Barney's lethargic, placated state of being was tactic acknowledgment of Conniff's right to exist. There was no higher validation that any human could ever possibly receive from a cat, and Conniff was receiving it in a highly visible public forum.

It was clear to all that Conniff had scored an indisputable victory, and it now seemed possible that he had finally earned the respect of everyone.

He hadn't. Not by a long shot. But, still, taking everything into account, this was a positive development for him.

CHAPTER THIRTY-THREE

The judge called a recess so that Ms. Mason's lacerations could be bandaged up. Conniff watched as the court stenographer tended her wounds. There was nothing overtly creepy about Conniff looking at one woman rubbing ointment on another woman's wrist; still, most observers couldn't help but believe that Conniff was saving this image for his spank bank.

The Judge called for a conference between himself, Mason and Conniff in his private chambers. He decreed that what was discussed would be private and not for public consumption.

But he did live-tweet it.

The following are the series of tweets he posted on his Twitter profile during the private, confidential, closed-door session:

I must say, Ms. Mason is an attractive young lady. The way that athletic gauze hugs her skin is a real turn on.

If loving her is wrong, I don't want to be declared mentally competent in a court of law.

Conniff has no idea that while he's making an impassioned plea on his own behalf, I'm listening to the *Kill Me Now* with Judy Gold podcast on my ear buds and not listening to a word he's saying.

Have you been watching that show on Netflix, you know, the one in the zeitgeist that everyone is talking about? Pretty awesome.

Which reminds me, listening to Conniff for just a few minutes is like binge-watching a crappy show for hours.

Ms. Mason is saying that the cats should get everything they're asking for. It raises a thorny legal issue -- how do I give this lovely woman everything she wants and still come off as all judgey and shit?

They're both making a strong case for their sides. The whole world is watching. I'd better make a wise and responsible decision.

Does live-tweeting a closed door hearing count as a wise and responsible decision? Probably not.

I mean, confidential closed door sessions contain too much complexity and nuance for a Tweet. A blog would be the better way to go.

The judge stopped tweeting and dismissed Conniff and Mason so that he could deliberate and make his decision. Neither Conniff nor Mason had formally concluded their cases, but the judge had come to believe that the American Judicial System had become too dependent on form and structure and a more freewheeling, avant-garde approach was needed, with less reliance on quaint, outdated concepts like reason and protocol.

But all this was mainly a question of style. As was always the case in these moments, he took his sacred duty as a judge in a court of law very seriously, and he approached the task at hand with a deep sense of urgency.

But first he checked his Twitter feed to see how many retweets he got.

It was rather disappointing. The most retweets for any of his tweets was 12, and he only got 27 "likes." He was a man of enormous professional stature, but as is often the case with people on social media, the paltry accumulation of retweets and "likes" made him feel like a complete failure as a human being.

He became despondent and didn't feel like he even had the emotional strength to go back out into the courtroom, much less give a measured and thoughtful decision in the case. He later told this reporter that he just wanted to go home, watch *Golden Girls* reruns and eat ice cream.

He aimlessly scrolled through the Internet for a few moments when he came across a video of two cats sharing a bowl of milk. One cat pulled the bowl of milk towards her with her paw and then drank from it, then the other cat pulled the bowl of milk towards him with his paw. They kept doing this over and over again. It might not sound that great on paper, but the sight of this simple behavior was delightful and it made the judge instantly feel better. Then, when he retweeted it, and immediately received over fifty retweets and a hundred "likes" in less than two minutes, he was downright giddy. And for the first time, he felt maybe just a little bit of empathy with Conniff and understood the motivation behind using cats to build up your social media presence. Most clinical psychologists agree that approval from strangers on Twitter and Facebook goes hand-in-hand with building up your self-esteem, but the judge never knew until this moment how true that was.

Nothing renews a person's zest for life quite like sitting alone in a room and staring at a computer screen. That is what happened to the Judge. Feeling completely reinvigorated, he returned to the bench to render his decision.

CHAPTER THIRTY-FOUR

The room was hushed as the judge got ready to speak. The only noise you could hear was the rhythmic cadence of Millie and Barney snoring (it was a much softer, smooth jazz variation on Conniff's snoring). It was perhaps the most important moment of their lives but they had no interest in being awake for it.

Although not snoring, Conniff was exhausted from his day of being a lawyer. All of that incompetence can be quite tiring. He was having trouble keeping his eyes open. Whatever Conniff's attributes, he has never had much of a talent for consciousness.

Ms. Mason was wide awake and eager to hear the verdict, not just because she was anxious for victory, but also because her allergy medication was running low and her prolonged proximity to Millie and Barney was giving her skin and eyes a decidedly *Walking Dead* veneer.

Everyone in the court listened with rapt attention as the judge spoke:

"I have been presiding over this case with great interest for most of the morning and part of the afternoon," he said. "Whatever the merits of the arguments both sides are making, there is no doubt that the two cats in question, Millie and Barney, act like the world owes them a living."

This was a surprising statement for him to make. It came off as somewhat belittling of the cats. The snark that Ms. Mason had been railing against when it came to Conniff was now detectable in the judge's voice.

Ms. Mason's face fell, at least the part of her face that hadn't fallen already due to allergic infection. For the first time, she had the feeling that maybe the judge was going to rule against her.

"I hereby decree that the cats will not be awarded the damages that they seek."

Ms. Mason covered her mouth. She felt slightly nauseous, but she didn't want to throw up because there had already been enough of that in the courtroom today, thank you very much.

"Instead," the Judge continued, "I have ruled that henceforth the world will officially owe Millie and Barney a living. All business and corporations are now required to hire them for any job they may apply for. And any human who comes in contact with them is obligated to cater to their every whim, no questions asked. They are legally owed it."

Then, with great aplomb, he banged his gavel and added the catchphrase he closed all his trials with, "Court is adjourned."

CHAPTER THIRTY-FIVE

When a judge rules that the world now legally owes you a living, you would think that this would be a life changing event. But since the end of the trial, Millie and Barney's life has changed not at all. Being that they are house cats with an aversion to leaving the apartment, an aversion made even worse by their day in court, they never ventured out to any place of business to demand the livings that were now owed to them. Instead they returned to their routine of sleeping, eating, sleeping, peeing, sleeping, crapping, sleeping, looking at things, sleeping, eating, etc, except now they did it with just tiniest bit more sense of entitlement. It was subtle and hard to notice, but it was there nonetheless, particularly in the way they did everything in exactly the same way as they always had.

So basically, their relationship with Mr. Conniff was on par with before. He fed them, sheltered them, cleaned up their waste and petted them under previously negotiated terms. Millie and Barney allowed all this to happen, and when they expressed their disapproval of Mr. Conniff, it was not by means of scratching or causing him physical harm. Instead, they criticized Mr. Conniff with passive aggressive methods familiar to all cat owners - they tore apart his sneakers, stood in the litter box while urinating outside the litter box, and stared at him for hours with accusatory looks of burning resentment. And as before, they never failed to whine and treat him as the enemy during the minute and a half between the time he opened the can of cat food and the time he got the food into their bowls. Conniff was grateful for this state of affairs. Like all cat owners, he couldn't imagine a daily routine that didn't involve sharing a home with creatures who belittled and begrudged him everything.

It seemed as if all had returned to normal. But then, in a shocking development, it turned out that Millie and Barney were not yet finished with the legal system.

CHAPTER THIRTY-SIX

It came as a huge surprise to legal observers when Millie sued Barney for plagiarism. Ms. Mason took up her case, and if she was worried about any animosity between her and Barney, she put those concerns aside because after much careful contemplation, she decided that Millie's case had merit.

"I was skeptical at first, but after looking into it, I was quite certain that this was a clear case of intellectual property theft," she told me.

And what ideas of Millie's did Barney steal?

"It's a whole litany of blatant acts of plagiarism," Ms. Mason said, presenting a list taken from her legal brief:

1. Sleeping on top of the suitcase that Mr. Conniff always left on the floor was Millie's original idea. But the day after she first started doing it, Barney claimed the top of the suitcase as his own and then abusively pushed Millie away when she tried to sleep there, even though there was plenty of room for both of them, and it was all Millie's idea in the first place.

2. One afternoon, while grooming herself, Millie began bitting her nails as if she was trying to pull them off, but she was really just aggressively cleaning them. Barney saw this and started pulling at his nails in exactly the same way. When visitors to the apartment saw Barney doing this, they all commented on how cute it was, but Barney never gave Millie proper credit for doing it first.

3. Sitting in the bathtub for no good reason. Millie did it first. Barney commandeered this idea to the point where the tub was never available when she wanted to do some pointless sitting.

4. *Taking a huge dump in the litter box just as Conniff was going to sleep at night. Both cats delighted in the knowledge that the stench forced Conniff out of his bed, with no choice but to scoop big wet turds from the box at the exact moment when he most needed rest. This habit of late night bowel movements was one of the most effective tools in Millie and Barney's ongoing Operation Annoy Conniff campaign. Millie came up with the idea, then Barney commandeered it as his own and even went so far as to claim that he was the true auteur of their turds.*

5. *Millie was the first cat in the apartment to start sticking her head into paper bags and then shaking adorably to get out of them. She was also an innovator in the field of peering out from inside cardboard boxes.*

Barney, according to Millie, blatantly stole all these ideas.

And Millie found it particularly galling that when Conniff began posting videos on the Internet of Barney executing all the adorable ideas that he had stolen from Millie, Barney seemed to embrace the attention and celebrity that resulted. Soon Barney had his own Twitter feed and Facebook page, and one time Millie witnessed Barney pawing at Conniff's iPhone, and she could have sworn that he was on Tinder, trying to swipe right with his paw.

And all of this Internet stardom was being sought by a cat that had once sued its owner for exploiting him on social media. This caused Millie to lose all respect for Barney. She now considered him a total sell out.

These were serious charges leveled by Millie against Barney, and the trial between them promised to be one of the most contentious cases in legal history. Nothing could stop it from happening.

Except for that thing that stopped it from happening.

CHAPTER THIRTY-SEVEN

The trial never happened because on the day of what was supposed to be her first deposition, Millie spent the entire morning staring out the window and completely forgot about what her issues with Barney were in the first place. Barney also tuned out and didn't give much of a shit either, and it didn't even seem to bother Millie that not giving a shit about plagiarism was an idea Barney stole from Millie.

THE END

CHAPTER THIRTY-EIGHT

The publishers of this book have informed the author that an upbeat, syrupy, saccharine, heart warming happy ending is required for a book about cats, so please disregard the insertion of the words "The End" at the end of the previous chapter.

It has been pointed out by the publishers that the most successful books about pets always have a feel-good vibe about them that this book just doesn't have. In *Marley and Me*, for instance, the animal at the heart of the story dies, but this book has no such fatality so therefore it doesn't have the uplift that a tale of this sort requires. It is a bit challenging to add even a spoonful of sugar to a story about two self-centered, mean-spirited narcissists (three, if you count Conniff), making the task of tugging at the heart strings all the more daunting, especially when you consider that Millie and Barney would quickly grow bored with tugging at heart strings before tearing the heart and the strings to shreds.

But this author is open minded about creative changes to a book, because of a deep belief in literary flexibility and also because it's the only way to get the final installment of the money I have coming to me. So what follows are sincere albeit desperate attempts at a Syrupy, Saccharine, Heart-Warming Happy Ending.

CHAPTER THIRTY-NINE

Syrupy, Saccharine, Heart-Warming Happy Ending -- Attempt # 1:

In the days after the Cats v. Conniff trial, the judge and Ms. Mason began dating. They are now married and Ms. Mason is expecting their first litter.

Ms. Mason was worried that she might experience an allergic reaction to the judge, so she was relieved to discover that this was not the case, unless you consider love an airborne illness.

The judge was as drawn to her as she was to him, and the romance between the two grew like a tree. Eventually, the judge marked his territory on that tree, writing the words "I Love You" with his own urine.

THE END

CHAPTER FORTY

Unfortunately, the publishers have deemed the conclusion of the previous chapter an unsuitable happy ending, despite the author's assurances that the part about peeing "I Love You" onto the tree of their romance was strictly metaphorical. In most cases, ending a story with a romantic couple living happily ever after is as surefire a happy ending as you can conjure up, but focus groups have revealed that as respected as the judge is on a professional level, people are just plain creeped out by him on a personal level. It's not that he engages in canine cosplay -- furries are generally nice people who just happen to have this particular thing they're into -- but the problem with the judge is that despite his denials, he has never really been housebroken. There have been multiple incidents and this fact alone may ultimately be the reason why he has yet to be considered for a Supreme Court appointment.

CHAPTER FORTY-ONE

Syrupy, Saccharine, Heart-Warming Happy Ending -- Attempt # 2

Much to Mr. Conniff's surprise, the official end of the trial brought to him the potential for romance. Moments after the judge had banged his gavel, the court stenographer approached him.

"I just wanted to apologize for the way I behaved," she said. "In the throes of a trial I always get all stressed out and I act out in ways that are not representative of who I really am. Tossing the transcription machine at your head, biting your ankle, acting the way I did, there is no excuse. It was so wrong and I am so, so sorry!"

She looked directly into Conniff's eyes as she said this. There was a genuine warmth and a kindness that shone through, and her smile was like a hug from love itself. There was something about her that was so welcoming, a quality that made you think you could happily hold her in your arms for the rest of your life.

But, alas, now that she didn't seem like a crazy unhinged psychopath, Conniff was no longer attracted to her.

THE END

CHAPTER FORTY-TWO

You don't have to tell this author that the previous chapter was not an adequate happy ending, so we'll try again. (And I fully acknowledge that this chapter kind of sucks, too.)

CHAPTER FORTY-THREE

Syrupy, Saccharine, Heart-Warming Happy Ending -- Attempt # 3

In an email to this author, the court officer wanted it known that he ranked 17th in the "Funniest Bailiff in New York" competition at Dangerfield's in Manhattan, and he did request a mention about his upcoming stand up gig at QED comedy club in Astoria, Queens (further investigation revealed that this was an open mic). Since that particular engagement happened days after the trial but several months before this book's publication date, we felt that telling you about it would cause limited harm to the general public. And not to brag, but withholding information about an open mic earned us a commendation from the Tri-State Area Good Citizenship Council.

Mr. Conniff also asked if his website and social media pages could be mentioned in this book so people can find out about his upcoming events and appearances.

This seemed like a reasonable request, considering that he's one of this book's main protagonists.

But ultimately the answer was no. No way.

THE END

CHAPTER FORTY-FOUR

The author and the publishers had a big argument over the previous chapter. Concluding the book on a refusal to help Conniff promote his career struck me as a the very essence of what a happy ending should be, but the publishers disagreed, so there is no other choice but to beat on, boats against the current, borne back ceaselessly into the past. (This right here strikes me as a pretty good way to end a book, but apparently it's been done already. Whatever.)

CHAPTER FORTY-FIVE

Syrupy, Saccharine, Heart-Warming Happy Ending -- Attempt # 4:

You might expect to hear a story of heroism about a dog saving someone from a dangerous situation, but in all likelihood, you've never heard such a yarn about a cat.

Well, nobody expected Millie and Barney to rescue a kitten from a burning apartment.

And the last thing anyone ever expected Millie and Barney to do was work in tandem as a team to collectively prevent what otherwise would have been a tragedy to instead be a triumph of the human spirit facilitated by two cats on behalf of a tiny little kitty.

And certainly no one ever expected the entire city of New York to join together in a celebration of gratitude towards two unlikely cats who redefined what heroism is in the twenty-first century.

Well, if you weren't expecting that, you were so right, because none of it -- not the fire, not the kitten, not the rescue, not the celebration -- ever happened. Are you friggin' kidding me? These are two cats we're talking about. Jeez, get a grip.

THE END

CHAPTER FORTY-SIX

Okay, the previous chapter obviously doesn't even come close to the up-beat ending we're talking about. The only explanation that can be offered is that the strain of working on this ridiculous story is starting to wear on the author.

Apologies.

CHAPTER FORTY-SEVEN

Syrupy, Saccharine, Heart-Warming Happy Ending -- Attempt # 5

The satisfying outcome to this book has finally arrived, because this reporter went to his mailbox this morning and was delighted to discover that the check for the final installment of his advance had arrived and he's already been to the bank and the check cleared. So if you're still hoping for some contrived tacked-on happy ending to this book, well, screw you, I got my money!

THE END

CHAPTER FORTY-EIGHT

Alright, wait a minute, although a bureaucratic error on the part of a publishing company has enabled the livelihood of this reporter to no longer be dependent on an upbeat assessment of cats, it is also true that after being around many cats in the course of reporting this story, and in the course of my career as a journalist covering the house cat beat, there is something undeniably true that I have learned about them, so here it is... Syrupy, Saccharine, Heart-Warming Happy Ending -- Attempt # 6:

People love cats.

Cats don't often return that love, and "don't often" is another way of saying "almost never." Cats are in it for the food and the bed and the shelter and the litter box. That is what they expect from humans, and if cats are willing to softly purr during a belly rub or squeeze up against your leg, it is never about you, it is always about them. And yet...

People love cats.

Humans spend millions of dollars a year taking care of them, and if a cat gets sick and the human dips into his or her savings to provide medical treatment, the cat complains loudly as it's being taken to the vet and makes it as difficult as possible for the doctor to give them care and then offers no gratitude to anyone for all the trouble people have gone through to make them feel better. And yet...

People love cats.

They place them in their laps and in their arms and pet them and talk to them in an affectionately infantile way. They look to cats to comfort them in times of crisis, heartbreak, tragedy, depression, and loss. Many cats will sit still as a human cries about their lives, but being of comfort is of no comfort to them, they're in it for their own coddling. You may see yourself as a gentle soul who is reaching out to a fluffy animal as a way to feel a little less lonely in this harsh, unforgiving world, but the cat just looks at you as a can opener and a sanitation service that can never unionize or go on strike. To a cat, you are a necessary annoyance, a hoop they have to jump through without ever having to jump or even get out of bed if they don't want to. And yet...

People love cats.

Under the right circumstances, a human being will leap, cat-like, at the chance to give someone love. When it happens with another human being, it is as good as it gets; however, human-on-human love is quite complicated. But despite, or maybe because of, all their psychotic behavior, loving a cat is effortless. In fact, amid all the insane nonsense you have to put up with, loving a cat might very well be the easiest part of having one. So it's perfectly understandable that people are prone to having one or two living in their houses and apartments. People love snuggling and holding and hugging and rubbing those soft, cuddly creatures called cats.

But don't rub them the wrong way, or they will sue your ass in court.

THE END
(For real this time.)

Made in the USA
Columbia, SC
29 November 2017